THE PRODUCT MANAGEMENT INTERVIEW

How to Find the Right Job as a Product Manager and Crush the PM Interview Process

By Alex Willen

© 2019 Alex Willen. All rights reserved. No portion of this book may be reproduced in any form without permission from the publisher, except as permitted by U.S. copyright law. For permissions contact: alexwillen+books@gmail.com.

CONTENTS

Title Page	1
Copyright	2
Introduction	5
Paths to Product Management	9
How You Are Being Evaluated	22
Finding the Right Company	38
PM Interview Questions - Experience	42
PM Interview Questions - Design	71
PM Interview Questions - Problem Solving	92
PM Interview Questions - Homework	107
Questions From You	127
Recruiter Phone Screen	129
Hiring Manager Phone Screen	132
On Site Interview	136
Conclusion	154
Glossary	156

INTRODUCTION

So you want to get a job in product management. First off, let me say kudos - product management is incredibly challenging but equally rewarding. You'll find yourself with an enormous amount of responsibility but also the ability to make a serious impact on your company in a way that few others can.

The bad news is that product management jobs are tough to get, even for experienced PMs. Many of the skills needed to be a PM are soft and hard to evaluate - things like communication, organization and empathy. That, combined with the fact that making a bad hire on the product team can be gravely detrimental to a company, means that even great candidates can get rejected.

That's a problem for both sides - good people may not be getting jobs where they would excel, and companies miss out on the opportunity to make great hires.

Ultimately, that's why I decided to write this book. Not knowing how to prepare properly can cost a candidate a job, but it can also cost a company a potentially fantastic product manager. I can't give anyone the answers they need to get hired as a PM if they aren't qualified (many of the questions you'll get are about your experience, and it's tough to fake answers to those), but I can help with the presentation.

Much of the interview process for product managers is about past experience, but having that experience isn't enough. You must be able to talk about that experience in a clear, organized way that highlights the skills your interviewer is looking for. That's what I'm here for - to help you understand what interviewers are looking for and how to answer their questions in a way that conveys your product management skills.

Over the course of this book, I'll go through a few topics related to getting hired as a PM. First, I'll go over the big picture - what roles there are in product management and what each of them are responsible for, as well as what hiring managers are looking for during the interview process. Next, I'll go through the types of questions you should expect, with numerous examples and my detailed thoughts on how to structure your answers. Finally, I'll talk about the other half of the evaluation process - how you should evaluate the companies where you're interviewing. The process is a two way street, so just as it's important that you have good answers for the interviewers' questions, it's equally important that you ask the right ones and think critically about the answers you're getting.

One of the topics I'm going to discuss later in the book is all the different types of product managers out there. There are PMs at early-stage startups and Fortune 500 companies, just like there are PMs of simple consumer apps and PMs of complex enterprise security products. Each of those will have very different experience, despite the fact that they're all product managers.

With that in mind, my background is in product management at early-stage enterprise software companies, where I've spent over a decade learning the ins and outs of PM. I joined Box when it was 50 people, Blue Jeans when it was 200 and Talkdesk (where I was the first product hire) when it was only 40. Most recently, I was the Senior Product Manager at UpCounsel (a marketplace for legal work) responsible for our product's core user experience. That means I've been lucky enough to see what successful, fast-growing companies look like starting early on. It also means that I have more experience with hiring at small companies than very large ones.

I've been on both sides of PM hiring interviews - I've interviewed hundreds of candidates and have been a candidate quite a few times myself. Both experiences have taught me plenty by giving me opportunities to see how other interviewers and candidates handle the interview process. I've seen people who come off as incredibly impressive, and some who I had to cut off early because it became clear very quickly that they wouldn't be a good fit.

Even so, my experience has only exposed me to a relatively small number of companies. That's why I've also spent countless hours talking to other people in the tech industry. I have spoken to dozens of product managers, but also recruiters, CEOs and engineers. All of them have different perspective on what it means to be a great product manager and how to hire one. I'm always looking to learn more, so if you have thoughts on this book, product management or anything else, I hope you'll reach out to me at alexwillen@gmail.com.

With that, onto the book - let's get you a job in product management!

PATHS TO PRODUCT MANAGEMENT

One of the questions I'm most frequently asked about product management is how I got into it. This is a constant source of curiosity for people in tech both because product managers are very visible within any organization, which creates curiosity about how they got there, and because there's no standard answer. Talk to a hundred product managers, and you'll get a hundred stories of how they got into product management.

If you want to be in sales, you get a job as an SDR (sales development representative - the lowest level of sales employee) out of college and work your way up. There are similar paths for support, marketing, finance and engineering - just get an entry level job, do good work and get promoted. In product, though, there are very few jobs available to new grads, which means most people have to find other ways to break into product. Perhaps the most common path is through internal transfers, but that's not the only way. I was hired as a PM despite not having any direct product experience, which is possible but a bit less common.

If you've decided you want to be a PM, know that it takes patience, skill and good relationships to actually get a product job. The fact that there's no roadmap is actually quite apropos. After all, when you're a product manager, there's no roadmap except the one that you create. It's a job that requires out of the box thinking and lots of soft skills, and you'll need those things to land the role in the first place.

There are really three ways to get hired into your first product management job, and in order from least to most common they are: getting hired as a PM based on related experience, getting into a rotational program or entry level PM role and transferring onto the product team from another role in the same company. Let's explore each of those and how to make them happen.

Getting Hired Based on Previous Experience

This is what I did, and if I'm being totally honest there was a lot of luck involved. The reality of getting your first PM job this way is that you have to have some other related and useful experience, but that isn't enough. You also need to have a hiring manager who thinks that your experience is useful enough to make you worth training on core PM skills and who has the time to actually do that training. Even if your background is highly relevant to a company, if they need someone who can drop in and get up to speed as quickly as possible, you're not going to be a good fit.

One thing to bear in mind here is that depending on where you are in your career, you might have to take a step down in level for your first PM job. If you're a senior marketing manager, for example, it's unlikely you're going to get a senior PM role - regular PM is much more likely. The good news is that PMs are on the very high end of the pay scale, so even if you take a lower title, you probably won't have to take a pay cut.

I've seen four categories of people get hired into a product management job without any direct experience: those coming from related tech roles, people with a few years of experience in traditional high-skill, high-prestige jobs (e.g. top-tier consulting and investment banking), newly graduated MBAs and those with industry experience.

Coming from Tech

This is my experience, and while it's not something that you see often, it's not shocking to see someone come over from a related role like product marketing manager or more execution-focused roles that often fall in the product domain, like project and program managers. In all of these cases, you have people that have worked closely with product managers and understand what successful product managers look like. Their skillset is relatively close to that of a product manager - the big difference is that their experience lies in execution, not strategy and roadmap planning. This isn't to say a role like PMM can't be strategic, but the type of strategic responsibility is different.

This background means that these types of people can start to contribute quickly as product managers, since a significant part of being a PM is execution. With the right manager in place, they can learn the more strategic side of things over time, but their existing skills make them relatively low-risk hires for product management.

Note that I haven't included engineers in here. While it's possible to go from engineering to product, in my experience it happens much more often through internal transfers, which I'll discuss shortly, than between companies.

If you want to go this route, it really helps to get a warm introduction to the hiring manager from someone they trust. When a recruiter is sifting through a stack of applicants, they're liable to throw out the ones that don't have any PM experience. Getting straight to the hiring manager with a recommendation that makes her believe that you're going to be able to apply your existing skills and pick up what you need to quickly will at least help you land an interview. Reach out to friends and former colleagues when you see their companies have openings for product managers. You should also probably not bother with senior PM roles - those are going to need that strategic experience that you won't have had yet.

Coming from Other High-Skill Jobs

I've worked with a number of product managers who came from consulting and a few that came from investment banking, and they've generally been successful. There are a couple of reasons hiring managers will consider these people: first, these jobs serve as excellent gatekeepers, because everyone knows they have very difficult hiring processes and require long hours of difficult work. If you've put in a couple of years at Bain, BCG, Morgan Stanley or Goldman, it's generally a pretty safe assumption that you're a smart, capable person, and you're willing to work your butt off. All of those are signals that you might make a good product manager.

Second, those types of jobs have skills that overlap with some product management jobs. If you're an investment banker, you've spent lots of time building models and analyzing data, which is really helpful at large consumer companies. If you're working at Twitter or Facebook, your decisions as a PM should be driven by the data available to you, and not everyone can capably sort through the amount of data companies like those have in order to draw meaningful conclusions. The analytical nature of a growth PM might be a good starting point.

If you're coming from consulting, you've spent time understanding the needs of your clients and crafting solutions for their business problems. This isn't so different from being a product manager at an enterprise software company, where your roadmap is going to be driven by your customer needs. It also doesn't hurt if you're comfortable working with high-level execs of clients, since you'll be spending some of your time as a PM on sales calls for the most strategic deals.

Different companies will have different perspectives on hiring people with these kinds of backgrounds, so it's always helpful if you can connect directly to someone at the company (especially the hiring manager) to understand what kind of culture they have and what type of people they hire. If you can't do that, though, check out LinkedIn and see what people's resumes look like. If there are already product managers who have the same kind of experience that you do, then recruiters will likely see your current position as a positive and will want to chat with you.

New MBAs

Getting an MBA is the most structured route to becoming a product manager, but it's also polarizing. Some hiring managers love MBAs, and others are automatically predisposed against them. I don't have strong feelings on the topic, but I lean a bit towards the latter camp. I've worked with both very good and very bad product managers who came out of business school, and the reality is that they tend to be more suited for some PM jobs than others.

Fresh MBAs often have the opposite challenges of people who have worked in PM-related fields like program management - they have a great head for strategy but little experience actually handling execution. In small startups like those I've worked in, this can be a real problem. Those environments need everyone to be able to get stuff done. There's no one to delegate work to, so there's no value in planning a strategic initiative if you can't make it happen.

At larger companies, this tends to be less of a problem. As companies grow, roles tend to become more specialized - there's no need for a jack of all trades when you have a whole team with a diverse skill set. You may find room for product managers here who can focus squarely on strategy while leaving execution to others.

If you want to go the MBA route, you should work to tailor your MBA experience to be as relevant to product management as possible. Many programs offers PM tracks and classes, so look for these when you're applying and making a decision about where to attend. Make these the focus of your MBA, and you'll show hiring managers that you've used the resources available to you to prepare as effectively as possible for a product manager role.

During your MBA summer, try to find a product management internship. These exist at plenty of larger tech companies and some startups, and if you're at a top-tier school, they'll be on campus recruiting. If you have your eye on startups that don't have MBA intern roles listed, it's still not a bad idea to reach out to the hiring manager. A thoughtful note that shows that you're genuinely interested in the company and are eager to add some value for the summer will often get you a coffee meeting.

The surest way to have a PM job lined up at graduation is to get an internship and do a great job. While interns are useful, half the reason (and arguably more than that) for the program is to try out prospective PMs.

Industry Experience

This is the least common role into product management, and that's because it requires you to switch from some other industry into tech, which few people do. A few examples of what I mean:

- A general contractor joining a company that makes technology for the construction industry
- Someone in the entertainment industry joining a company like Hulu or Netflix
- A medical student moving into a medical tech startup

While these people bring few of the directly relevant skills for a product management role, their domain expertise can be so valuable that it's worth hiring and training them anyway. The challenge here, as with some of the paths above, is making the hiring manager believe that you can pick up those core PM skills.

For this reason, your best bet for making this kind of a move is to network with product managers and find those at companies where you have relevant domain expertise. Go to product manager meetups and other groups (there are plenty in the Bay Area and lots of online groups for those living elsewhere), and talk to PMs from companies whose products you feel that you could contribute to. If you can speak intelligently about the challenges they're facing, you're on the right track.

They won't necessarily have product roles open immediately, but you can still offer yourself up as a resource, since it's always helpful for a PM to be able to ask questions of someone facing the problems they're trying to solve. When a product role opens up, if you're seen as a helpful, intelligent person with useful domain expertise, that will go a long way towards getting you the job.

Rotational Programs

There aren't a lot of rotational product management programs out there, but if you can get into one, it's one of the most straightforward ways to get into tech. They're typically targeted at people earlier in their career (some look for people straight out of school, while others might want 2-3 years of professional experience). The reality is that these programs tend to be run by large companies with lots of resources, so they're looking for potential more than experience. It's a lot like getting an entry-level job in banking or consulting - there's no expectation you'll have experience, because they're going to teach you what you need to know. Rather, they're looking for people who can keep up with a fast-paced learning environment and pick up the skills they need.

For these programs it never hurts to know someone at the company, but most people just send in a regular application. They run on different schedules, so keep track of who's hiring when and get your application in early.

One thing to bear in mind is that many of these programs are for entry-level associate product manager jobs. If you're coming out of undergrad, that's fine, but if you're more experience and looking to make a career change, you may have to take a pay cut, at least in the short term.

Here are a few rotational programs to get you started:
- Facebook Rotational Product Manager Program
- Twitter Rotational Associate Product Manager Program
- Uber APM Program
- Workday Rotational Product Management Program
- Kleiner Perkins Product Fellows Program

There are also broader rotational programs designed for new grads to get a taste of multiple departments within a business, and these typically include a stint in product. They're not as focused, but you'll get some good product experience and other great exposure as well.

A few examples:
- HubSpot Leadership Rotational Program
- Microsoft MACH Program
- Visa New Graduate Development Program

These are great places to get your career started if you're coming right out of undergrad.

Internal Transfers

One of the most common ways people move into product management is by transferring to that team from elsewhere within the same company. There are a couple of reasons this makes sense. First, when you consider what hiring managers are looking for (which I'll get into in more detail later in the book), many of those skills are difficult to evaluate in an interview setting. Things like leadership and communication can be tough to suss out in a structured, 45 minute discussion. On the other hand, when you have a chance to work with someone every day for months or years, it's very apparent whether they have these skills or not.

Beyond that, anyone who already works at your company is going to have relevant domain expertise. They know your product, your users and your coworkers. If they're in marketing, they've helped to craft the external communication of your products. If they're in support, they've helped to troubleshoot issues with your products and bring feedback to the product team in the form of bug reports. If they're in engineering, they've been building your product. This means that they have a level of expertise that you can't get from outside the company.

The fact that in this case the hiring manager knows you and has had a long time to evaluate your experience means that there's less risk in hiring you than someone with comparable experience from outside your company, which is why an internal transfer is a great way to get your first PM role.

Still, just because you're already at a company doesn't mean you're as shoo-in for a product management job. You need to make sure that your product team knows who you are and sees the good work you're doing. For that reason, it's important to put yourself in a position where you're working with product. Luckily, product works with just about every department, so there will usually be a way to get that face time with the PMs.

Let's take a look at how you can build towards a product management role from a few different departments: marketing, engineering, sales/customer success and support.

Marketing

In many software companies, you'll find product managers and product marketing managers (PMM) tied at the hip, because each one's success depends on the other. A PMM needs a good product, or the quality of marketing won't matter. A PM needs good marketing, because it doesn't matter how good your product is if no one has ever heard of it.

This makes marketing a good place to start on the road to product management, especially for people who don't have the technical background to go into engineering. As a PMM, you'll have close relationships with the product team and will be embedded into the later stages of the product process.

If you want to go this route, just make sure you focus on the product marketing side of things (as opposed to things like brand marketing and lead generation). This will allow you to work closely with the PM team. Once they see you as a valued resource, let them know you'd be interested in moving over to join product - even if there isn't a spot immediately, there may be opportunities for you to expand your product responsibilities while remaining on marketing, so you'll have the experience you need to make a seamless transition when they are ready to add to the team.

Engineering

Transferring from engineering might be the most common route into product management. There is no team that works more closely with product, and engineers are instrumental not only in building products, but also in providing technical feedback that is key to critical product decisions.

If you're in engineering, you should have frequent exposure to your product team during standups, sprint retrospectives and other planning and coordination meetings. Use this time to engage with your PM and provide technical feedback that helps to drive decisions. As a product manager, there's nothing I love more than an engineer who will proactively give me technical suggestions on ways that I might change a feature or alter the scope of a product in order to deliver it more quickly.

Try to become the go-to resource for PMs who need input on technical questions. Sometimes I have a thought about something we might build and absolutely no idea the level of technical depth. In those cases, I want to get a quick technical gut check from an engineer - is what I'm proposing something that's likely to take two weeks or two years? That sort of input can save me from wasting time on planning something in detail, only to find out its infeasible when we have an estimation meeting.

For those questions, I've almost always had one or two people on my team I rely on - sometimes it's my team lead, but often it's just the engineer most eager to put on his product hat. If you're that engineer, you're going to get great exposure to the product process and build a tight relationship with your PM. If my product-minded, valued engineering counterpart tells me he's interested in moving over to the product side of things, you bet I'm going to push to make that happen.

With that in mind, it's important to mention that one of the biggest challenges that former engineers have in product is letting go of the technical details. Once you're a PM, your job isn't to figure out how to build things (or to build them) - it's to figure out what to build. Some former engineers have a tendency to write product specs that include technical details on how things should be built, because it can be difficult to get rid of that instinct. Remember that while PMs and engineers work closely together, their roles are very different. Make sure that you're willing to give up some of the technical work you're doing if you want to make this move.

Sales/Customer Success

I'm combining these two because they work with product in very similar ways. If you're building enterprise software, sales reps and customer success managers provide an invaluable connection to customers, both pre- and post-sales. Every PM should be engaging with customers, but you can't talk to all of them. That's why a good product manager will keep a small circle of folks on each of those teams to act as a sounding board that represents the broader customer base.

If you can be one of those trusted resources, you'll build a good relationship with your product team and can demonstrate that you understand the product development process. The best way to get a PM's attention is to use what you have - customer information. If you're on the sales side, help your PMs out by categorizing requests from prospects. Keep a list of everything each customer asks for that you don't already have in the product, along with the name of the customer, their potential deal size and anything else that's especially relevant to your business. Most sales reps don't want to spend time doing this, so it really stands out when you put forth the extra effort. If you can catalogue this information not just for your own deals, but also those of your colleagues, you'll quickly earn the gratitude of PMs.

The same applies to customer success. A customer success manager (CSM) is constantly engaging with customers and hearing about what's working well, what's not and what new features they'd like to see. Collect and categorize this information, or better yet work with your manager to build out a system that all CSMs can use to do so.

Remember, if you're in a customer facing role, you have information that is valuable to product managers. If you give that information to them in a way that will help make better decisions, they'll treat you as a resource. At that point, they'll be more than happy to answer your questions about product management and let you know what you can do that will put you in the best position to join the team.

Support

I have known a few great product managers that started their careers in tech support. Their dealings with customers gave them insight into the products that they were able to parlay into PM jobs down the line.

The way to go about this is very similar to sales and customer success - if you're in support, you have useful information from customers that is valuable to the product team, so take advantage of that. Many companies have someone from support meeting with product management each week or two to represent their team. They provide feedback on bugs that have arisen and get information from product on what is going to be fixed and when, which they take back to the team. If you can get into that position, PMs will see you as a valuable resource.

One thing that I've seen some senior support reps do to stand out is to customize their support software to help suit the needs of product. A tool like Zendesk has a wealth of information about the product, but a PM doesn't have time to go through thousands of individual tickets. If you can help create a system in which tickets are tagged so it's easy for a PM to search for all issues related to a particular feature or product, you'll make her life much, much easier. Talk to your PMs about what information they can't easily get about bugs, and make that information easy to get. Once you've done that, you're in a great position to help define the process by which product works with support.

Everyone

Whether you're in one of the above groups or not, there's a trick to learning more about product management and understanding what you can do to put yourself in the best position to become a PM. This one is a closely guarded secret, but I'm going to let you in on it. Ready?

Go to a product manager at your company and say "Hey <product manager>, I'm really interested in product management, and I'd love to learn more about it. Can I buy you coffee/lunch/a drink and pick your brain?" PMs are generally friendly people who are happy to chat, so this is an almost foolproof approach. We also like free food, and many of us need coffee to survive.

Once you've got one on one time, ask the product manager how he got into product management. We PMs love to talk about ourselves, so this is a great starting point. After that, ask if there's anything you can do to help out the product team from your current position. We PMs also love people who make our jobs easier, so this is one of the most reliable ways to start building a relationship that can lead to a product job down the line.

HOW YOU ARE BEING EVALUATED

If you want to impress your interviewers, first you have to know what they're looking for. You may be a great PM, but if you're interviewing for a position whose main responsibility is big-picture strategic planning on social media software and all you do is talk about how good you are at writing extremely detailed product specs for network switches, you're probably not going to get the job.

That's the first important point - the interviewers are evaluating you, but they're also evaluating your fit for the particular job. The more experienced you are, the more the fit is going to matter, which is why you want to convey not just that you have done all manner of important things in your product management career, but also that you've done similar things to what will be expected of you in the role.

With that in mind, let's first discuss some general characteristics and skills that interviewers will be looking for in most PMs, then we'll move onto some more specific role-based ones.

I mentioned that more experienced PMs will be judged more on fit, which also means the reverse is true - if you're interviewing for a junior PM role, a good interviewer will understand that you don't have much experience and will instead try to judge whether your personality and skills are a good fit for the PM role generally.

Soft Skills

Here are the most important things that they'll be looking for:

Communication

An enormous part of being a product manager is communicating. You have to communicate with customers and users to understand what's working well in your product and what isn't. You have to communicate with people who aren't customers yet, but who you'd like to be, to see what you need to add to your product to get them to use it.

You need to communicate with design and engineering in order to let them know the requirements for products and features. You need to communicate with support to ensure they know what your products are supposed to do and how to deal with issues that arise. You need to communicate with sales so they know how to sell your products. You need to communicate with marketing so they get the message right.

You get the idea - communication is a constant part of life as a PM, which means it's important that you be able to communicate clearly and intelligently.

Interviewers will evaluate you on your communication skills two ways - specific questions and general behavior. You may get questions like "What do you think should be in a PRD?" which ask specifically about how you think an important piece of communication should be structured. Beyond those, though, it's important to understand that your communication skills are being judged throughout the entire interview.

Every time you answer a question, you're communicating, so every question is an opportunity to judge your skills. This is why, especially when it comes to questions about your previous experience, you must be able to talk in a coherent, organized fashion. You should be able to tell the stories of previous work you've done in a way that answers the specific question being asked and has an appropriate amount of information.

Don't leave anything important out, but also don't ramble. Be as succinct as possible while still making your point, then end your story. Many interviewers will stay silent for a few seconds after you're done, whether on purpose to see if you'll continue or just because they're taking notes. Don't worry about this - you know what you're saying, so when you're done, stop and wait for the next question.

It's incredibly important to practice your stories - that way they come off as well-organized and you come off as confident. That said, ensure that you're answering the question. Interviewers can tell when you're just shoehorning a practiced anecdote into a question where it isn't really relevant. Sounding confident is great, but not if you aren't answering the question.

If you get something unexpected, stop and think about it. See if you can adapt one of your existing stories to answer it, and if not come up with something else out of your experience. Do take the time to think about it, though - pausing for ten seconds to think is much better than rambling or giving an irrelevant answer.

Organization

This is going to be something for the more junior roles - if you're interviewing for a VP of product job, it will be assumed you're organized enough to handle it based on your prior experience. For an associate product manager (APM), though, organization (along with communication) is critical. If I'm hiring an APM, I'm trying to find out if that person can be relied upon to take work off of my plate, and that means I need to ensure they're organized enough that they won't lose track of their responsibilities.

As with communication, organization can partially be assessed by the way you answer questions. This is doubly true of anything you're doing on a whiteboard - when you have a broad question to answer, or a hypothetical question about what you might do in a particular situation, ensure that you answer with a clear framework that you explain to the interviewer.

One good example of this is a question we'll discuss further in a later chapter - "You're working on X, but someone tells you that Y needs to be handled immediately." Part of what I'm looking for when I ask this question is a well-organized response about your options. If I'm asked it, I always explain that I have three things that I can work with - scope, time and resources - and then I go through each of the three to discuss how they are relevant to the particular question.

You may also be asked questions about non-PM experience. If you're transferring to product from another department, these may be about your work there. If you're a customer success manager, I'll ask you to tell me how many customers you are responsible for and how you keep track of your communications with all of them. Similar with sales - I'll ask about how you manage your leads and how you choose to organize your time to close the most deals.

If you're coming out of school, you may get questions about group projects or other work that you've done. You may even get questions about your schedule that seem very casual (e.g. "Wow - it looks like you're doing a lot between all your classes and clubs! How do you manage all that?"). While they are casual in that they're designed to get you comfortable by having you talk about something you're very familiar with, they're also assessing your organizational skills.

Don't tell the interviewer that you forsake sleep and a social life to keep up with all your activities, and don't just shrug nonchalantly and say you manage to make it work. Talk about how you plan out your class schedule and how you divvy your time up between outside activities. You want to come across as someone who appreciates the boundless opportunities that college offers and thus takes the time to pick the right classes and activities to take advantage of the experience.

Prioritization

This is the essence of the PM job - can you take a bunch of disparate information from different people with different perspectives and turn it into an organized list of priorities, while being able to justify those priorities?

This one will get tested by your experience and by hypothetical questions. We'll get into these in much more detail in a future chapter, but for now the most important lesson to understand is that you always need to be able to clearly explain why you've prioritized in the way that you have and that you can defend your decisions.

If asked about prioritization choices you made in previous jobs, try to focus on ones that you're sure you got right and that you are very comfortable defending. Ensure that you can answer several levels of "whys" - if you're asked why you prioritized X and your answer was that it would bring in a lot of revenue, you need to be able to answer why you think it would bring in a lot of revenue.

Collaboration

Do you work well with others? I certainly hope so, because if not a PM job probably isn't for you. It really boils down to working with people both inside and outside of your company at all times, so your interviewer will want to make sure you work well with others.

Part of this is just a general assessment of your personality as you interview. The common term for this is the airport test - if you were traveling with this person for business and had to spend several hours with them at an airport on a layover, would you be okay with that? Everyone wants to work with people they like (you are spending eight hours or more a day with them, after all), so needless to say you should be pleasant to your interviewers and anybody else you encounter, whether it's the CEO or the receptionist.

Beyond the general assessment, though, there will also be questions specific to how you engage with other people. These will frequently come from your hiring manager as well as those in other departments who want to know how you would work with them. A head of design will often ask how you like to work with design - same for an engineering manager and engineering.

These questions are partially subjective - some engineers just want a perfectly detailed spec they can build with as few questions as possible, while others want to come on customer interviews and get all the business context possible for what they're building.

If you want to give the answers the interviewer is looking for, try to understand the organization and how it works. If you're dealing with a small startup, people probably want to be more collaborative. In those cases, the engineering and design managers probably want to hear that you think their departments are on equal footing with product and that you like to treat engineers and designers as true partners, not people you dump work off to. In a bigger company, the focus may be more on nailing all the details of formal communication documents, so that nothing gets missed when you hand those off to other teams.

My recommendation here, though, is to really understand how you like to work with other departments and stick to your guns. I genuinely do want to treat engineers and designers as partners - I love to get designers into customer interviews with me, because they'll ask different questions than I. With engineers, I'm happy to defer to their preference - I've known some who love firsthand context and others who want me to get all the info and just give them a succinct document - but I do prefer to have at least one person on the engineering team I can bounce big-picture ideas off of early on, so she can tell me if what I'm talking about is technically infeasible before I go down a rabbit hole.

If you stick to your opinions here, it'll cost you some jobs, but those are the jobs in which you won't be a great fit anyway. If you like to work with your colleagues in some particular way, better to be transparent about that from the beginning, so when you get a job offer it's from somewhere that you're excited to be every day.

Experience Level

Particularly as you interview for more senior roles, your interviewers will be trying to determine if you have specifically relevant experience for the role.

In terms of level of experience, this is the general progression of PM roles:
- Associate Product Manager
- Product Manager
- Senior Product Manager
- Group/Principal/Staff Product Manager
- Director of Product
- VP of Product
- Chief Product Officer

There are plenty of variations and related titles - you may have seen directors or heads of platform/growth/other product-related areas that live in the product organization. Nonetheless, they'll all be comparable to one of the above titles in terms of types of responsibilities.

As you move up in seniority, the job becomes increasingly strategic. An associate product manager makes very few decisions - instead, she is primarily handling execution. She should be able to identify the relevant stakeholders for a task and communicate with them, and she should be able to provide well-organized resources and updates to the rest of the PM organization about her areas of responsibility.

A chief product officer, on the other hand, does not handle execution (except at the smallest of startups). Her responsibility is to guide the direction of the product at the highest levels, considering business strategy more than the details of the roadmap - those can be left to lower-level leaders in the product organization, and the execution can be left to individual contributors.

Here is a brief guide to what interviewers will be looking for at each experience level:

Associate Product Manager

As mentioned above, an APM is there to handle execution. Her responsibilities revolve around making the decisions of higher level PMs happen, as well as communicating updates about the day-to-day progress of her areas of responsibility.

The APM role is often part of a training program - while APMs can be incredibly helpful in their own right, the ideal candidate is also someone who can learn the skills to move up to a PM role. Thus it's helpful to have some understanding of product management while interviewing (i.e. know what Agile is, understand what more senior PMs do), it's not as critical as showing that you're a hard worker who can execute on a daily basis.

Product Manager

At this level, the PM has some strategic responsibilities, though usually just within his area. Often the product leadership will really decide what the company's strategy is and what products are going to be built, while the product manager is assigned to focus on a particular product within that strategy.

Generally, a PM will handle the short-term roadmap for his product, while much of the longer-term direction will come from above (though the PM will certainly have input into that direction).

When you're interviewing for a PM role, you need to show that you can handle all of the day-to-day PM work of communication and prioritization. Beyond that, you can set yourself apart by showing strategic thinking about product as a discipline and the industry of the job you're applying for.

Senior Product Manager

A senior PM has a role similar to that of the product manager, but is generally someone who has shown she can think at a higher, more strategic level and make meaningful contributions to the larger roadmap.

When I'm evaluating a senior PM, I'm looking for someone who can be given high-level guidance and trusted to develop a roadmap and execute it with minimal guidance.

To land a senior PM job, you'll need to demonstrate that you're experienced in independently managing a product. You will generally need to be able to talk about products that you've been fully responsible for since they launched. Building incremental features isn't enough - if you're a PM looking to move up to a more senior role, work with your manager to take responsibility for a whole product.

Group/Principal/Staff Product Manager

In larger organizations, you'll see individual contributor product roles that go above senior product manager. This can also be the case at smaller startups, but it's much less common. Individuals at these very senior levels are going to be highly trusted, highly experienced product managers who can be counted on to build out the strategy for a product (or in the case of group PM, a group of related products) and ensure that strategy gets executed.

These PMs will not have direct reports, but they'll generally be seen as leaders within the organization. They will often have the help of more junior PMs and serve as mentors to them. A PM at these levels will be directly responsible for the success of his area of the product and the business.

To get hired at this level, you need to show that you can not only handle all of the core PM responsibilities with minimal oversight, but also that you're a leader. You need to be able to exert influence on the direction of the roadmap despite, so come prepared with anecdotes about the impact that you've had on previous organizations.

Director of Product Management

This is where the responsibility changes significantly - all the previous roles have been individual contributors whose main purpose was to manage a product. Once you hit directory, the primary responsibilities are now people management and strategy.

A director of PM will have PMs reporting to her, and she'll be responsible for their work as well as their career development. She will also be responsible for helping set the product strategy. In larger organizations, it will be up to her to gather all of her PMs thoughts on where resources should be invested and what the company should be doing and represent those to the executive team.

The step up to director is a challenging one to make, since it's the first role that requires people management. If you're a senior PM looking to make this step, try to find ways to get some management experience. If your company has a product internship program, volunteer to run it (or if there isn't one, volunteer to start one). If you have APMs, see if you can start managing one of them.

VP of Product Management

The vice president of product is one step above a director. In some organizations, especially smaller ones, a VP will have individual contributors reporting directly to him. In larger organizations you'll find a more traditional structure - individual contributors report to a director, and directors report to the VP.

Beyond managing his subordinates, a VP of product management will be responsible for strategy, either for the whole product or a significant area of it if there are multiple VPs. He will generally have P&L responsibilities (i.e. ensuring the product is making money and managing its costs) and significant latitude to design strategy and process within his management area.

Chief Product Officer

Only a minority of companies have a CPO, but if you have one, she is responsible for product at the highest level. She will report to the CEO, but if a CPO was hired it's because the CEO deeply trusts her to manage the company's entire product strategy.

She will manage the senior leaders in the product organization directly and be fully responsible for everything related to product. She will also likely contribute heavily to product-related areas like marketing.

Domain Expertise

When assessing your fit for a product role, hiring managers want to make sure that you can not only handle the responsibilities of the level at which you're being hired, but also that you will be able to effectively work on the type of product their company is building.

There are many different points of view on the importance of domain expertise - some people think it's critical to have experience with the type of product you'll be managing, while others (myself included) would rather hire smart, adaptable PMs and let them figure out the details of what they're building over time.

There is a certainly a credible argument to be made for domain expertise, especially in particularly complex products. The skills needed to build a social game for iOS are very different than those needed to build a network security product. There is always some overlap - both jobs will require the core communication and prioritization skills - but if a job requires you to understand specific ways of doing business, technical concepts, legal regulations or anything else industry-specific, a PM who comes in without knowing those things will require more time to ramp up than one who has already experienced them at a previous job.

With that in mind, as you're considering which jobs to apply for, take this into consideration. It doesn't hurt to apply for roles in areas where you don't have an enormous amount of expertise, but try to do some reading about the industry beforehand and come up with parallel experiences that you can reference from previous jobs.

As an example, I have interviewed at some consumer-focused companies despite my expertise being in enterprise software. In these cases, I point out that at all of my previous companies, while we have certainly had to handle enterprise security and administration requirements that aren't present in consumer software, we've also been very focused on consumer-type design. It's been the belief at all the companies at which I've worked that it's not enough for a product to check all of IT's boxes - it must also be something that will be easy for the people who have to use it on a day-to-day basis to understand.

One of the best pieces of advice I can give is to understand the background of the people who are interviewing you. Especially in product, people tend to hire people with similar backgrounds. If you look up an interviewer on LinkedIn and see that he's been working at software companies that serve one specific vertical for his entire career, he's probably going to place a lot of emphasis on having experience in that vertical.

On the other hand, I've jumped around to PM jobs at companies making software for very different purposes, so I look very favorably upon PMs who have demonstrated that they can learn and adapt. I've done lots of on the job learning and have been successful, so I know it's possible and that biases my preferences accordingly. Try to use your interviewers' experience to get a feel for what kind of person they're looking for - that will help you focus on the right areas of experience.

With that in mind, let's dive deeper into the different types of PM roles that are out there and the skills and background hiring managers will be looking for in each. Note that many of these will overlap - a growth PM will likely be working on frontend parts of the product, for example.

Frontend

A frontend PM will be working on user-facing areas of the product. This might be an iOS app, a web app or some kind of device, but the most important thing is that it's what users will be interacting with. Thus, a frontend PM needs have above-average design and user experience skills. He should be able to work meaningfully with design and should have experience interviewing and getting feedback from users of previous products.

Backend

A backend PM is managing systems that are behind the scenes. This is usually a more technical role, since a backend PM is responsible for the services powering the user experience. If you're applying for this job, you don't necessarily need to be a former engineer, but you'll need to be able to have technical conversations and understand technical requirements.

Expect to get a lot of questions on working with engineering and your previous experience working with complex systems. You should be able to talk at a high level about scaling infrastructure and security issues. If you're an engineer looking to move into product management, this kind of a role may be a good starting point, since you'll have much of the relevant domain expertise from your engineering experience.

Growth

The growth PM is an interesting role that's almost a hybrid product/marketing position. As its name implies, this role is generally responsible for growing some part of the business (usually users).

Because the growth PM often doesn't own a specific part of the product, she needs to work with other PMs to help them optimize their own product areas. This means that soft skills like communication or collaboration are particularly important.

If you're coming from a marketing background (especially marketing ops or other analytics-heavy roles), you should have plenty of relevant experience to draw on when interviewing for a growth PM position. Be prepared to answer questions about funnel optimization, both your past experience and hypothetical problems.

Generalist

You'll really only find generalist PMs in early stage companies - once you've had time to grow out a team, it's more efficient for PMs to specialize. If you're relatively young to your PM career, I highly recommend trying to find a more generalist role at somewhere early stage (though to be clear, they don't call them generalist PMs, but if the company and PM team are small enough, any PM is effectively a generalist) - it's a great way to get exposure to lots of different types of products.

When interviewing for very early-stage product managers, I'm always looking more for ability to learn and adapt than specific PM skills. Since both the team and the company will be rapidly evolving, it's more important to convey that you'll be able to roll with the punches as things change than it is to show that you're a perfect fit for what the company is doing at that particular moment.

Internal Tools

A lot of product managers cut their teeth on an internal tools role. It's a good way to get PM experience without being in a position to put out products that aren't good for users. Your stakeholders will be your colleagues in the company, so it's easy to get their feedback and talk to them about changes you intend to make.

Internal tools include things like billing systems, user management tools and other internally-built applications. A food delivery company will have an order management system they've built in house, while Facebook has internal tools to help manage spam and fake accounts. The job is very much a traditional PM job, you're just working on things that will be used in your company, not by end users of your company's product. That means it'll likely be a more junior PM role and thus interviewers will be looking for experience on the core PM skills.

Platform

The word "platform" gets thrown around a lot in tech these days, and people use it to mean all kinds of different things. Usually, though, a platform PM is going to be someone responsible for APIs and other related products. This is usually going to require a more technical background, since the end users are going to be software developers.

If you're transferring to product from an engineering role, a platform role may be a good place to start. An experienced engineer will likely have experience both creating and working with APIs, and knowing the product both as a developer and a user is very helpful in terms of domain expertise.

Mobile vs. Web

In many cases, product managers' responsibilities within a given company are divided up based on the platform the product is being served on - that is, for a small company, you may have one product but a PM who manages the web version of it, a

PM who manages the iOS version and a PM who manages the Android version.

This structure can work well because each of those areas requires different engineers, has different requirements and really acts as a standalone product. There will be a product leader who will be responsible for making sure there's consistency between them, but it's also important to make sure that you have an iOS PM who is up to date on the latest iOS design conventions and the rules for dealing with the Apple App Store.

If you're interviewing for a specific iOS (or Android or another platform) product management role, you'll need to have some specific expertise. If you're technical, it helps to have built apps for the platform (whether professionally or for fun). If not, you should still be able to point to your experience managing apps on that particularly platform and speak intelligently to the latest developments on it.

Enterprise vs. Consumer

This is another important distinction, though unlike the platform one, this will show at the company level - you don't have enterprise and consumer PMs at the same company; it's the company that is either making enterprise or consumer software.

As I've mentioned, my background is in enterprise software, which means I have more experience dealing with issues like security and user management in my products, plus I have expertise working with sales to engage with prospective customers. On the flip side, I have less experience with consumer design, with scaling applications to handle hundreds of millions of users and with funnel optimization.

Conclusion

Before we move on, I just want to reiterate here that every PM job is different, as is every interviewer. If you're applying to jobs that are out of your immediate area of expertise, do everything you can to prepare to explain the holes in your experience and why they won't stop you from doing a good job. Pull in experience from non-PM roles to show how you have skills that will help you succeed if necessary.

Also remember that people are going to want to hire people whose resumes look like theirs. Try to get a sense of what people value from their experience (and if you're willing to put in the time and effort, check their LinkedIn and Twitter accounts to see if they're posting anything you can learn from).

Lastly, find out what they're looking for by asking. I'll cover this more in a future chapter, but I always ask the hiring manager what he thinks a successful candidate will look like. This is especially useful if you have a phone screen with him before going on site - if so, he'll happily tell you what he wants in a candidate, so use that to your advantage in preparing for future interviews.

FINDING THE RIGHT COMPANY

Now that you have a basic idea of how to make your way into product management and what roles there are, it's time to discuss the next step - finding the right roles within the right companies.

I've said before that product management differs greatly between companies, depending on their size, industry, product lineup and history. So how can you find the ones that will give you the experience you need to stay motivated and continue developing in your PM career? Thankfully, today we have enormous amounts of information about prospective employers that you can use to your advantage.

Your Company

As I've mentioned, many people transition into product via an internal transfer in their current company. Their domain expertise gives them immediate value, and the fact that the PM team already knows them makes them less of a risk to hire.

That's why it's always best to start with your employer - go talk to the PM team, understand how they're organized and get involved in whatever way you can. Even if you don't find a role, it will give you a real life example of what a PM team looks like and how it functions.

Network

If there isn't a PM job available for you at your company, the next thing to do is try your network. Reach out to people you've worked with before - both those who are in product and those who might be able to make an introduction (engineers, designers, execs, etc.). Don't push for a job immediately; instead, let them know you're looking to learn more about product management to see if it's a good fit and that you'd love to take some folks to coffee and pick their brains.

If you can set up coffee, lunch or even a phone call, use the time to learn about product management, how people got into it and what they like and dislike about it. After you get that feedback, though, try to steer the conversation to a job. Explain that you know that it's tough to make a transition into PM, and you're looking for entry level jobs. Ask how they evaluate prospective candidates, and see if you can get feedback on your experience and how you might improve it to make yourself a great PM candidate.

If you feel like the conversation is going well, ask if their company has any entry level PM openings or if they know anyone at companies that do. Remember to keep an eye on the time, so you're not making this ask hurriedly as your time is running out. Don't feel intimidated - many companies offer bonuses for referring candidates (which can be as high as $10,000 for a product manager), so generally folks will be happy to send your resume in.

Searching For Companies

There are plenty of ways to find companies with PM openings, but first you should evaluate what it is that you're looking for. Because it's hard to find a first PM job, you should optimize this not around your preferences, but instead around your experience. Look for places that have a reason to give you a shot, even if they're not in your ideal location or industry. The most important thing is to find a PM role - once you've got some experience under your belt, you can be more choosy about your employer.

I recommend starting with companies in your industry. For the same reason your current employer would value your domain expertise, so would your employers' competitors. If you understand the industry and the competitive landscape, you can start adding value much more quickly than someone who has to get ramped up. This means that even if you're competing with someone who has direct product management experience, you still have a chance, since it may be just as much effort for that person to learn a new industry as it is for you to learn product management.

If you don't know your competitors, there are plenty of places to look. I recommend:

- https://www.crunchbase.com/ is a database of venture-funded tech companies, and you can search through it by industry, amount of funding and a number of other characteristics. This can be a very useful tool for quickly building a list of companies to look at.
- https://angel.co/ is similar but has smaller (including very early-stage) startups, if that's what you're interested in.
- Many publications put out lists of top companies to work for every year - you can easily find these by googling "Top startups to work for in <city>" and "Top tech companies to work for in <city>". These are obviously a bit less targeted than a filtered search on Crunchbase or Angellist, but you may find some great prospects nonetheless.
- Read tech news! If you're following TechCrunch, Hacker News, Product Hunt daily, you'll constantly hear about new companies

Company Sizes

In general, I would recommend that you don't worry about company size - if you get offers from both small and large companies then it should play a role in your decision among them, but at first you might as well apply to both.

That said, there are some differences to consider in your approach and how you're finding them. With large companies, you're more likely to find rotational programs or true entry-level PM roles. Because they have the resources to train people, they will be the likeliest ones to have roles with no PM experience requirement. Focus on the ones that have these job postings - it's unlikely that they're going to open up a new role for you, so spend your time on the ones that are already there.

Smaller companies lack the resources to spend time training people, but they do have the flexibility to create roles for someone they're very excited about. For these companies, your network is going to be much more important - the right people vouching for you can make all the difference. If you know founders or execs at early stage startups, try to find out what problems they're having and position yourself as the solution. You may not end up with a PM role exactly, but you might be able to find a position that allows you to help out with PM work as it comes up, so you can make that move down the line.

PM INTERVIEW QUESTIONS - EXPERIENCE

If you interview for PM jobs, you'll hear a whole variety of different questions. Some will be cliche ("What's your biggest weakness?") and others will be designed to get some information while being fun ("If you had a superpower, what would it be?"), but ultimately, the goal of all of them will be to assess you as a candidate.

We've already talked about what your interviewers will be looking for as they evaluate you, and this section is about how they get that information. Some interviewers will be better than others, but regardless of who is talking to you, you'll come across as a better candidate if you've prepared for their questions.

There are really two types of questions - those that are trying to evaluate your personality, and those that are trying to evaluate your experience. It's not tough to tell which is which; the ones trying to evaluate your experience will ask about what you've done in the past or ask you hypothetical questions about how you would respond to a particular situation. Pretty much everything else is there to assess your personality.

The experience questions are the ones that you can truly nail with the right preparation. You should have a set of stories about your previous experience that you've practiced thoroughly and can recite when a relevant question comes up. Even if you're a highly experienced PM who's done it all, selecting the anecdotes you plan to use before your interview is the best way to ensure that you tell them in a logically-structured, well-organized manner that makes you come across as both experienced and collected.

My goal here isn't to give you specific answers to questions you may be asked, but rather to give you an understanding of why they're being asked and what you're being evaluated on. Since your experience is unique, your answers will be too; just make sure that you're not just telling stories, but also conveying the qualities that interviewers are looking for.

Tell me about yourself.

This one's easy, right? There is literally not a single human being on this earth who has more expertise on the topic of you than you.

Yes and no - on the one hand, you do have all the info you need to answer this question. On the other hand, you need to be sure you give the right information in an organized way. If you spend five minutes talking about your childhood, your interviewer is going to perceive (correctly) that you are not a particularly effective communicator.

Have a good answer to this question prepared in advance that highlights information that's relevant to the job. My stock answer is that my background is in product management at early-stage enterprise startups. I started at Box, where I was employee number 50 (this is as good a time to name drop people/companies as any) and since then I've held a couple of product roles at other early-stage enterprise companies. My last job was at Talkdesk, a cloud-based call center software company) where I was employee number 40, the first product hire and responsible for our integrations with services like Zendesk and Salesforce, though due to the size of the company, I also managed several other product areas over time, including our billing system and our call routing system. I also launched two new products, including our first SMS product.

My goal here is to convey a few, specific things. First, I've worked at successful companies from very early on, so I've seen what a fast-growing startup looks like and can bring that expertise with me. Second, I've had significant responsibility, both in managing meaningful product areas and launching new products from scratch. Third, I've been in enterprise software for my whole career - that demonstrates relevant domain expertise for other enterprise software companies.

Once I interviewed at a company in the real estate technology space, so there I added that on the side, I run a small real estate investment group that owns residential properties in Oakland and Berkeley. That tells them that it's a particular area of interest for me, so I'm clearly joining for more than just the paycheck. It also tells them that I have domain expertise that is very specifically relevant to what they are doing.

When you're crafting your answer to this question, first figure out what you want to highlight in your career. I talked earlier about what companies are looking for in a prospective product manager, and this is your chance to highlight those things. Once you know what you want to convey, build a brief story that is in a logical order. Don't hesitate to bring up hobbies and side projects that are relevant - if you're interviewing at StockX (a marketplace for high-end sneakers) and you've been a sneakerhead since you were 10, you should absolutely mention that. If you're interviewing at an enterprise software startup, though, you can probably keep your love of sneakers to yourself.

Before you go for an interview, consider your answer to this question and how it fits the company. Just as I add my outside real estate experience when it's relevant, you should add anything that might be particularly helpful for a company to know. You may also want to remove details - if I were interviewing at a consumer company, I would leave out the fact that 100% of my product experience is on enterprise software.

Tell me how you would deal with two different stakeholders inside your company with opposing views on what you should be building.

As a product manager, one of your toughest but most important responsibilities is making the call on what gets built and what doesn't. Different people across the business will always have different and conflicting views - the head of support is going to think tackling bugs is the most important thing, while the head of sales is only going to care about closing deals. As a PM, you have impact on both of them, so it's important not only that you can be decisive about whose needs are a higher priority, but also that you can explain your decision to both of them in a way they'll understand and respect, even if they don't agree with it.

I like to tackle this question from two directions - the ideal and the practical.

The ideal is that by the time this conflict arises, you already have a company-level framework of objectives in place to handle it. On a recurring basis, generally yearly, your company should be setting objectives (often referred to as OKRs - objectives and key results). This process should take input from stakeholders in all departments of the company - sales, support, marketing, product, finance and anyone else who has an opinion about the future of the company. Your C-level executives should then use those inputs, along with their own opinions, to set high-level goals. There are a few types of these:

- Financial
    - Hit certain targets related to financial metrics like revenue, cashflow and margin
    - Increase ACV (average contract value)
    - Decrease churn
- Sales
    - Move up market and sell to larger customers
    - Sell to customers within a specific industry or vertical
    - Reduce deal cycle length

- - Increase percentage of deals won
- Marketing
  - Generate a certain number of leads or new user signups
  - Make a big impact at an important conference or trade show (as measured by leads generated from that show, press attention, etc.)
- Engineering
  - Reduce tech debt
  - Increase the ability of the product to scale to a certain number of users
  - Implement more efficient internal tools
- Support
  - Reduce the number of tickets opened about a certain issue or product
  - Decrease ticket response time
  - Increase customer satisfaction with issue resolution

As you can see, goals can vary significantly across the business - that's why objective setting should be led at the C level.

Once objectives have been set, they should be clearly announced to the company. It is also helpful to announce things that are *not* being set as objectives and why - this helps the stakeholders whose needs did not get prioritized to understand why not and to feel that their concerns were heard.

As a PM, you should then fall back on these objectives when stakeholders come into conflict. When your head of sales comes to you demanding a new feature to close a big customer and your head of support comes to you asking to prioritize bug fixes, look at your objectives - if the most important one is to reduce churn, you should remind your head of sales of that fact when you explain why you've chosen to prioritize bug fixes.

If the interviewer says, "That's fair, but what if your company didn't set those types of goals before that conflict arose?" then you fall back to your more practical answer. In this case, I like to start by giving both sides perspective - remind the head of sales that if you've got a horrifically buggy product, you're going to lose customers and develop a bad reputation, and that's going to make sales harder moving forward. Remind the head of support that while bugs are important, sales has to hit their numbers in order to pay the support team's salaries.

From there, assess each issue in terms of scope and urgency. How bad are the bugs that support wants fixed, and how big is the feature that sales needs to close the deal. Look at timelines - does sales need to close the deal before end of quarter comes in a few weeks? This is really just you going through the standard process of gathering relevant information and using that to prioritize issues. If you're at a small startup, you may want to escalate the issue as well - if you're talking about closing the biggest customer in company history, your CEO will want to be involved in the decision making process as well, and he'll have an opinion (which, realistically, will be the opinion that settles the whole thing).

After you've made a decision, the most important thing is to explain your decision, especially to the person whose issue you did not end up prioritizing. Even if it ended up that the CEO made the call, you should still do this, as it's a critical part of maintaining good relationships within your company. Talk about why you prioritized the other thing, and do so in big picture terms - what is the effect on the company, and why is that effect more important to long term success.

Use whatever tools you have to back this up and show that you've removed your own bias as much as possible - data is always a good one. If you can show your head of sales a Zendesk report that says the support team is getting a hundred tickets a day about the issue in question and that those tickets are taking up the time of two full time employees every day, that will help the head of sales to understand the scope of the problem. Similarly, if you have emails from important customers threatening to stop paying you if the bug isn't fixed, that helps too. Having this conversation will at least help your head of sales to feel like he was heard and his issue was evaluated in an objective manner.

Lastly, you should develop a plan for building what sales needs. People (especially executives) hate hearing no, but they'll be much more understanding if you tell them that it's just a no for right now, and you'll tackle their issue next month.

What was your product planning process like at previous companies?

I always ask this question when I'm talking to a candidate, because it's a great way for me to learn something during the interview. As a PM, I always want to find out more about what my peers are doing to understand how I can improve things at my company. Don't worry about trying to convey some particular aspect of your experience or personality here - the interviewer actually just wants to know how you did things in the past. This helps her know how easily you'll be able to learn their system (if you're used to planning three years out and you're interviewing at an early stage startup that can barely stick to a three month long roadmap, there may be some adjustment) and acts as a jumping off point for more questions about your experience.

I like to reinforce the fact that I always drive my product decisions based on company objectives, so I start there - at a previous employer, we did yearly company objective planning, followed by quarterly product roadmap planning and then bi-weekly sprint planning.

You should feel free to interject opinions on what you think worked well at your previous companies, what didn't work so well and your thoughts about process and how it should be developed. I take this as an opportunity to mention that I think process should be reactive - especially at smaller startups, you should wait for problems to arise and then create process to solve them. If you're too proactive about process you can create needless overhead and put things into place that don't actually solve real business problems.

I also like to talk about how I've seen (and helped) process change over time. This highlights a few important things about me - that I've worked at small companies that have grown quickly (and thus had to change process), that I'm not stuck in some system but rather have experience being versatile and agile, and that I'm a more senior PM who doesn't just execute tasks given to me but also considers the bigger business questions of how the team should operate.

Tell me about a time you launched a new product.

This is going to be a question for more senior PMs. The interviewer is both trying to ensure that you have been responsible for a product from the very beginning and that you understand all aspects of creating a new product.

First, here's the quick list of things that I want to make sure I cover in this question.

- The genesis of the product
- Your process of gathering information from stakeholders
- Creating a PRD
- Working with design and engineering to turn that PRD into designs and tech specs
- Preparing for launch
- Measuring success and making future changes

That's quite a bit of information to convey, but that's the point. Creating and launching a new product involves significant planning and communication with internal and external stakeholders. Your goal here should be to demonstrate to the interviewer that you understand all of the relevant steps in the process, that you've executed them before and that you can think through them in an organized way.

Genesis of the Product

Ideally, this should be a story of how you thoughtfully analyzed some aspect of your business, identified a valuable opportunity and convinced your peers and superiors internally that it was important enough to justify spending resources.

This can include customer conversations - maybe every time you go on site to visit a customer, you see them facing the same challenge, and that challenge is something related to what your company does. It can include feedback from sales - perhaps they're disqualifying a lot of customers because you're not addressing some particular need. It may come from market analysis - you could use your existing technology as the basis of a new product that opens you up to a new use case or vertical.

Whatever it is, it should demonstrate how you can think about the big picture of your business and use the people around you, both coworkers and customers, to understand how you can do more to fill customers' (and prospective customers') needs.

In many cases, the real answer to why you started building a new product is because the CEO saw it in a dream and was convinced it would be brilliant (or something else coming from high up the chain of command, in which you had no input). If so, fudge your answer - even if the initial idea did come from the CEO, you probably helped to shape and improve it over time, so focus on your role and contributions. If you make yourself sound a little more instrumental to the process than you were, no one will be the wiser.

Gathering Information from Stakeholders

Once you have an idea, you need to validate it. While this process differs from enterprise to consumer companies, it all comes down to engaging with the people who you think might use your new product.

As an enterprise PM, you should have an existing customer base that you should validate your ideas with. Even if the idea originally came from customer requests, you need to make sure that the product you're designing is something that will serve a significant enough portion of the market to be worth the effort. If you're hearing the same request from a bunch of customers, but all of those customers are from a specific vertical that doesn't represent a huge market for you, it may not be worth pursuing.

When I'm validating my ideas with customers, I like to go through a few rounds of interviews with the same customers. My questions during these rounds increase in specificity over time. At first, I ask broad questions and try to get the customer talking as much as possible - "Is X a problem for you?" and "How do you handle X now?" are good, high level ones to get people to talk about their problems and current solutions. This tells you whether there are real issues and if there are other tools already attempting to solve them that you should be looking into. After I've talked to a few customers, I'll create a deck with a high-level explanation of what I see as the problem and thoughts on how to solve it, then I'll take that to the same customers to validate that we're on the same page. If so, I'll then create a basic product spec and go back with that, to see if they think that my proposed product will work for them. Depending on the product, I may go so far as to work with design and engineering to create a very simple mocked-up prototype and get reactions from customers as they use it.

The goal is not to bias them towards your thoughts early in the process, but to really understand their problems and whether your solution addresses them in a way that is practical for customers.

If you're working on consumer products, you can certainly do similar work, just with individual users. This can include both individual user interviews to go in depth with a small number of people about their problems and your proposed solution, and it can include larger-scale tactics like surveys to get information that has less depth but more breadth.

Creating a Product Requirements Document

Everyone has a slightly different idea about what a Product Requirements Document (PRD) is, and at early-stage startups there may be no real concept of a formal PRD. All companies create something at least PRD-esque, though - a document that defines the features of the product that needs to be built (and if it's a good PRD, why it's being built and who it's being built for).

When discussing PRDs, you should tell the interviewer both what should and should not be in them. In my view, the PRD should answer three things. The "why" is background and business context on the problem that's being solved and what the company hopes to achieve by building this product. The "who" is personas of the people who are going to use the product. The "what" is the bulk of the document - it describes, either as a list of features or user stories, what the product must be able to do. This may also include wireframe mockups created by a tool like Balsamiq.

What the PRD should not include is the "how" - your job as a PM is to figure out what product needs to get built and what it needs to do. It's up to engineering and design to figure out how it gets built, and the job of the PRD is to convey the "what" and relevant context in such a way that they can figure out how to build it.

One last very important piece of a PRD is key performance indicators (KPIs). You've stated the objectives of the product, so you should also discuss how you plan to measure them. This is important both as a thought exercise (so you understand what the important metrics of the new product are) but also as a technical one. Engineering needs to understand what you expect to measure so that they can ensure that data goes into your internal analytics tools.

Working with Design and Engineering

After your PRD is ready, it should go to design and engineering (or possibly just the latter if it's a backend-only feature). They should then have the time to digest it and ask questions. At this point, I still consider the PRD to be a work in progress - while it should be complete before you give it to design and engineering, you should be open to their feedback.

Design may have thoughts on how you can change product features to provide a better user experience. If your PRD says there must be a signup page that gathers the user's name, email, age and birthday, your designer might suggest just implementing Facebook Connect to gather that information more easily.

Similarly, as engineering gives you information on the technical side of things, you may decide to make tradeoffs. In my experience, the most common example of this is that engineering will tell me that some relatively minor feature of the product is actually deeply complex technically and will require significant time to implement. In that case, I may cut that feature or try to substitute something simpler.

Once you've finalized the PRD based on this feedback, design should work to create high-fidelity mocks, and engineering should break down the product into technical tasks. Once that is done to everyone's satisfaction, you can start building.

Preparing for Launch

You may note that I'm not covering the process of building the product. If I'm asking this question, it's to see if someone is senior enough to handle a new product from soup to nuts, and that means I'm assuming they've spent enough time as a junior PM to have managed the day-to-day of implementing new features. That said, if there were any major hiccups or changes of direction during the implementation process, you should mention those (if you can do so in a way that shows that you added value).

Instead, I want to focus on the other responsibilities of a PM once a product is getting close to launch. You'll need to work with a few groups to ensure that everything goes smoothly.

First is marketing - if you want to announce your product (and you probably do, since you want people using it), you'll want to work with marketing. Depending on your company and the product, you'll want to start this process anytime from two weeks to two months before launch. You'll need to make sure they understand what is is the product is going to do and who it's targeted at, so they can craft a marketing plan, create collateral and integrate this product into any other relevant marketing work they're doing.

Next is support - you should provide them with the resources they'll need to answer incoming questions about the new product. At minimum, you should demo the product to them (and record that demo) and let them know who to talk to in the event that unexpected issues arise. I also recommend working with them on a process to ensure you get feedback on incoming issues - if you're using a tool like Zendesk, this can be as simple as asking them to tag every new ticket about this product, so you can easily find all of them.

If there are billing, contract or revenue implications, you'll need to work with finance and possibly sales. They may need to add new products to the billing system, create new contract templates or do other work to ensure that you're able to sell the product, so make sure to engage with them as early as possible, as these kinds of changes can take time.

If you're working in enterprise software, you'll need to train the sales team on how to sell. Depending on your company size and structure, this may involve working with marketing (they're often responsible for sales enablement), sales engineering or the sales team itself. It's important that even if marketing is responsible for sales enablement that you still be present and available to answer questions. You're the expert on the product, and you want sales to know that you're the face of it. They will get questions and feedback from prospects, and as an enterprise PM, you want to make sure that they know to direct that to you.

Post-Launch

In my experience, candidates frequently stop answering this question at the point of the product launch. That's a mistake - especially in these days of SaaS, the launch of a product is just the beginning. You should have a plan for measuring the success of that product and planning additional features, and you should talk through what you did post-launch as a result.

I mentioned that your PRD should have KPIs, and those should come back into focus now. Talk about how you created dashboards or reports in your internal analytics tools that measured your KPIs. If you hit those numbers, great. If not, talk about how you took all of the information you got post-launch to adjust the product to make it successful.

If your story ends with your product being a total success, you'll often get questions from the interviewer about what you would have done if that hadn't been the case. Often these will be in the form of hypotheticals - what would you do if very few users signed up after you launched? What if the product had lots of users, but they were only using a free version and not upgrading, so it wasn't making money? There are endless variations, but they're all basically the same question - when things don't work out with your product, how do you handle it?

As with all your answers, this should be well-structured. First, you should be talking about how you analyzed the problem. Depending on what it was, maybe you looked at data to determine the scale of the problem, or maybe you did interviews with customers who tried the product and didn't like it to understand their issues. Whatever it is, your first step should be to clearly identify where you went wrong initially.

After that you've identified the issue, you have to fix it. If the interviewer is just asking you a hypothetical, you may not know how to fix it, but you can always come up with something that follows from your analysis. Maybe you found out customers weren't aware of the new product, so you worked with marketing to advertise it better. Maybe you found out that customers were confused by parts of the UI, so you adjusted those. Whatever it is, it should be clear that you came to the solution from a clear, well-informed analysis of the problem.

Tell me about a time you made a significant mistake.

The reality is that every product manager has made mistakes - what the interviewer is looking for here is what you did once you had discovered you made a mistake and what lessons you've learned.

You'll have to draw on your own experience for an answer to this question, but I think the most common category of mistake for this question is misprioritization - you decided that X was higher priority than Y, and it turned out that Y was more important. It also doesn't need to be a comparison of two possibilities - if you prioritized a featured with the expectation that it was going to drive a significant amount of revenue and six months out from launch it's done $0 in sales, you misprioritized that feature, regardless of what your other options were.

You need to discuss five things here:
- What was the mistake?
- Why did you make the mistake?

- How did you figure out you had made a mistake?
- What did you do once you realized your mistake?
- What did you learn?

What was the mistake?

This is pretty straightforward; just make sure that you can clearly articulate it in a sentence or two. "I pushed for us to build a product that I anticipated would drive a significant amount of revenue, but it greatly underperformed my expectations and was later deprecated."

Why did you make the mistake?

In hindsight, you should know what went wrong. There are a few categories of common mistakes here:

- Insufficient information gathering - You didn't actually talk to current and prospective users about your product to ensure that it was something they would want.
- Bad information gathering - Maybe you talked to the wrong people or asked the wrong questions. A common example of this in early stage software is talking to the people who would be using your software, but failing to talk to IT, who needs to approve the software before it's purchased. That leads to building great software that you can't actually sell, which is naturally a problem.
- Bad execution - You did a good job of gathering requirements, but you still ended up building a bad product. Maybe you didn't convey those requirements well to engineering and design, or maybe you launched it prematurely for marketing reasons, which led to a bad reception.

Whatever you do, ensure that you place the blame on your own shoulders. If you say that you did a great job gathering information and created a perfect product spec but engineering didn't build it to spec, that's very obviously a cop out, and nobody wants a PM who is going to lay blame on others.

Besides, if that's actually the case, there's no way engineering should have been able to build the product incorrectly without you knowing early on. Remember, you're the product manager, so if something has gone wrong, one way or another you bear some responsibility. In this job, the buck stops with you.

How did you figure out you had made a mistake?

Ensure that you can discuss exactly why it became clear that you misprioritized things. Maybe you set targets for your KPIs that the product didn't meet. Even if you didn't set KPIs, you likely had some rough idea of what success looked like that your product didn't get close to. Alternatively, maybe customers who you expected to buy it turned out not to be interested.

Whatever it is, talk about data - whether your product wasn't producing enough revenue, leads, engagement or anything else, it should be quantifiable in some fashion, and it's important to show that your opinions about the success or failure of a product are well-informed.

What did you do once you realized your mistake?

More important than what is why - if you decided to deprecate the failed product, justify that decision by explaining that you analyzed the amount of engineering time it was going to take to support it moving forward and determined that it wasn't worth it relative to the amount of revenue it was bringing in and the opportunity cost of using engineering hours on it.

Obviously that doesn't have to be your answer, but the goal is to come across as having made a well thought out, informed decision. Maybe you kept it going with a smaller team. Maybe you merged it with another product. Whatever the reason, the why is as important as the what.

If there were users of the product and you deprecated it, talk about that process as well. How did you notify users? What did you do to help them migrate to a competing product or get their data out of your product? This is a great opportunity to show that you carefully consider the results of your decisions not only on the business, but also on your users.

What did you learn?

This should relate back to why you made the mistake. If engineering built something way off spec, hopefully you learned that you need to be in standups every day where you get frequent demos of any progress being made, so you can catch issues early on. If you didn't talk to the right group of people, then you should have learned a lesson about ensuring that you find out who all the stakeholders are for prospective customers. This doesn't need to be anything especially deep, just a reminder that you're always learning and improving.

Concluding

Once you've gone through, wrap everything up neatly. This should sound something like "So to sum up, I pushed hard for us to build X, which I suspected would drive millions of dollars of revenue during the twelve months after launch. Six months after launch, it had only driven $50,000 and was not on track to get anywhere close to the originally stated goal. It turned out that I had failed to consider some of the security implications of the product, because I did not get feedback from my prospective customers' InfoSec teams when I was doing research. I determined that we could put in the additional security features necessary in a relatively short amount of time given the right resources, so I worked with the head of product to secure those resources. After the security features were released, I worked with sales to go back to customers that had previous turned us down, and we were able to start closing deals of significant size quickly and exceed the original revenue targets."

As always, the key is to come off as clear and organized in your thoughts.

Tell me about a time you had to convince someone else of your viewpoint.

Before I started my first PM job, a very experienced PM who I respect deeply told me that being a PM is "all of the responsibility and none of the authority." That's the best description of the job I've heard, and it's the reason interviewers ask this question.

As a PM, you are ultimately responsible for the success of your product, which means that you need to have influence over design and engineering (to ensure it gets built well), marketing (because if no one has ever heard of it, it doesn't matter how good it is) and sales (if the reps aren't selling it, it might as well not exist). The problem is you have no direct authority over any of them. That means that when someone else is critical to the success of your product, but that person disagrees with you, you have to convince him of your point of view.

As with other questions, you'll need to search through your experience to answer this question, but whatever your answer, it's important that it convey to your interviewer that you have the tools to convince others of your point of view. There are a couple of ways to do this that work well for answering this question.

When you disagree with someone, there are generally two reasons why - either you disagree about the facts, or you agree on the facts but interpret them differently.

Use Data

If you disagree with someone on the facts, the best thing you can do as a PM is show them evidence that you have the right facts, and generally this evidence lies in the data. Perhaps your head of support came to you insisting that all his reps are telling him there's a huge issue that needs to be corrected immediately. You check your analytics tool and find out that it's not nearly as significant as they're saying, and you look at some of the bug reports only to find that there's a simple workaround. You show these things to the head of support, and he agrees that it's not as critical as he thought.

Change Their Interpretation

Maybe you're both looking at the same data but drawing different conclusions. You and another PM might be looking at the same problem but coming up with different conclusions on how to solve it. In this case, you want to explain to the interviewer how you communicated with the other PM in order to understand why she was drawing a different conclusion than you.

Maybe she was interpreting the data differently - she sees the same problem you do but interprets its impact differently than you. Maybe you've both seen similar problems in your past and have solved them differently, and you're each just drawing on your respective experience. The key is to talk about how you learned why the other person was coming to a different conclusion and then helped them to understand your interpretation of the problem in order to get them on your side.

What do you do if you are about to miss a deadline for a product launch?

Just about every product manager has ended up in this situation at one time or another, so it's certainly something you need to be able to deal with. There are two big things you need to do if you're not going to make a deadline: *communicate* and *mitigate the impact*.

Communication

Communication is one of the absolutely key aspects of being a successful product manager. You should be communicating early and often to anyone who might be affected by your product, and that's doubly true when something is going wrong.

As soon as you realize that there's even a possibility that you might miss your deadline, start communicating with everyone who might be affected. If your deadline is tied to an event where your marketing team is planning a huge announcement, let them know ASAP. If you've promised a feature to a customer by that deadline, let everyone involved in the sale and post-sales relationship know. If missing the deadline is a really big deal that might affect your company in a significant way, run things up the flagpole all the way to your C-level leadership.

Stress that you want to communicate as early as possible. That gives everyone involved more time to understand the consequences of missing the deadline and to explore ideas for ways to get the timeline back on track or mitigate the impact of the issue.

Mitigate the Impact

That brings us to the second step - once you've gotten everyone up to date, you need to see what you can actually do about the issue at hand.

Any time you're dealing with a product deadline, you need to look at three things: timeline, resources and scope.

First, let's look at our timeline. Why do we have a particular timeline for this product launch, and is there anything we can do to change it? If the product was promised to a customer by a certain date, perhaps we can give them a one-time discount in exchange for pushing out the delivery date. On the other hand, if we're planning to launch the product at a major event like Salesforce's Dreamforce or Apple's WWDC, we're definitely not going to be able to move our deadline.

If you can get more time, great - you may have solved your problem. If not, move onto looking at resources.

Let's say you're launching this product at Dreamforce come hell or high water. The company has staked its future on this launch, so it's the absolute highest priority. In that case, perhaps you can move some engineers from another team to help out with the launch in order to get it out on time.

This is one of the big reasons to communicate early if things start to go south. If your engineering management is aware that you might need help, they can start looking at resources early and figure out what options are available. If you don't have in-house engineers to spare, you may be able to hire contractors to help out temporarily.

As a product manager, you rarely have direct control over engineering resources, but when a time-related issue arises, one of the first things you should be doing is talking to engineering management, because they may be able to solve your problem by shuffling some folks around temporarily.

The last thing to look at, and the one over which you have the most control as a product manager, is scope. Maybe you can't build what you had originally planned in time for your deadline, but perhaps there are things you can cut or at least delay.

A real life example from my product career: my team was supposed to launch a product at Dreamforce, but it became increasingly clear that we weren't going to be ready in time. We couldn't do anything about the timeline, and there were no extra resources to spare, so it fell to me as a PM to figure out a solution.

Our objective at Dreamforce was to get as many leads as possible. We had hoped to launch the full product on the first day of the conference, but there was no way that was going to happen. At a conference, though, you don't really need the full product - people come up to your booth, get a demo and give you their information so you can follow up. You don't actually close any deals until days or weeks (or months) after the conference.

With that in mind, I cut scope for what we had to hit by the deadline to just the frontend of the product and enough functionality on the backend for a scripted, controlled demo. I shifted the rest of the work to right after the conference, and we were done just in time to sell our first customer (one who had heard about the product at the conference) a few weeks later.

To summarize the answer, if you're going to miss a deadline, first you should communicate as early as possible with all the stakeholders. Next, look at the timeline, resources and scope, and see what you (or other people in your company) can change in order to either hit your deadline or mitigate the impact of missing it.

Tell me about a product that you think is particularly well designed, and then tell me how you would improve it.

This is a very common question, which is great, because it's one you can be entirely prepared for. Some interviewers will give you more leeway than others about the product you choose - sometimes literally any product is acceptable, while others might want you to suggest a software app. Since everyone has a smartphone, I've been asked specifically about an app on my phone.

I highly recommend picking an app on your phone. It will likely work for all variations of this question, plus if you're in a live interview, you can pull it up and visibly demonstrate the things you're discussing, which is much more effective than trying to describe an app, especially if it's complex.

You should consider a few things when selecting an app to use:

- Complexity - You don't want to choose an app that's too simple (if you remember the app "Yo" that had its moment of Silicon Valley fame, it's a good example - all you could do was pick a friend and press a button, and it would send them the word "yo.") or too complex. You need it to have enough functionality that you can talk about what you think works well and what doesn't, but not so much that it's tough to briefly explain the app and what it does.
- Quality - If you pick an app that you think is absolutely perfect, you're going to have a problem when the interviewer asks you to improve it. If you're just asked about an app that you like, you should still choose something you can critique, as you're probably going to be asked to do that in a follow up question. On the other end of the spectrum, though, don't pick something absolutely awful - this is supposed to be an app you think is well designed.
- Audience - Pick an app that's appropriate to discuss with another product manager who you know little about. If you choose a coloring book app that your child loves, you might get blank stares from a 22-year-old tech bro on the other side of the table. Similarly, don't pick something that's built for a very specific group of people and requires their domain expertise. If you choose an app that allows for modeling of complex financial derivatives, you'll waste all your time explaining derivatives and never get to the app itself.

Once you have it in mind, select three things that you think the app does well and think about why you like them. Put on your product design hat as you do this analysis - you want to describe things that are well designed, not just stuff that you think is neat.

There are an infinite number of possibilities, but here a few things you might consider from a design perspective:

- Presentation of information - Does the app use colors, sizes, fonts and other visual cues to highlight the most important information to you? Does it understand what is relevant to you in different situations and ensure that you're always presented with something useful?
- Sharing - If it's a social app, does it do a good job of making it both easy and useful to share information with your friends?
- Navigation - Does the app do a good job of making sure that you always know where you are, how to get back to the main menu and how to navigate to any other screen you need? Can you get access all the functionality you need with a minimal number of clicks?
- Offline mode - Some apps do a great job of bringing useful information offline to give you a good experience even when not connected to the internet. Google Maps, for example, lets you download local maps so that you still have them even if you're in a foreign country and don't have access to the internet.
- Personalization - Just giving someone the ability to personalize an app isn't necessarily good design, but learning about the user and tweaking their experience to be as ideal as possible based on who they are and why they're using it can really enhance the experience of using an app

Like I said, there are an infinite number of reasons you might think an app is well designed. There are also thousands of app critiques all over the internet, and it definitely doesn't hurt to read the work of some mobile developers and designers to understand what they think makes for great design.

That said, don't just steal one of those and parrot back what someone else says. Your interviewer may have lots of follow up questions, and if you aren't talking about an app that you truly know deeply, it won't be tough for them to figure that out.

Now that you've talked about what you like about your app, the next question will be how you would improve it. I really recommend talking about an app that you use frequently for this reason - you're going to know it well and will have plenty of thoughts on what you'd change if you were the PM.

The key is to be able to clearly explain why you would make your change. Clearly define your objective with the change and why you think it will accomplish that objective. I recommend that you start from your own perspective as a user and talk about how it will improve your experience, then talk about how that would benefit the company that makes the app.

If you think the signup flow is bad, tell them that you feel your time is unnecessarily wasted by a cumbersome process and you would have a better experience if they reduced the number of steps involved. Don't forget to identify why your change would be valuable to the app developer - for example, in improving their signup flow, they'll likely increase the number of people who sign up for accounts and will thus have more users of their app.

Once you've described the change you would make and why, one follow up question that comes up often is, "Why do you think the company that makes this app hasn't done that already?"

Consider the company's objectives - have they built a social app that likely wants to maximize user numbers, or is it a relatively expensive tool designed for a specific market of users that they want to corner? Think about all of the possibilities and where the company is in its life - a social app may want to attract users at first, but once it has a large userbase, the company's objectives may change to focusing on monetizing the users that are there.

If you think about the example of a clunky signup flow, perhaps they're actually trying to weed people out. It costs money to support user accounts, so maybe they want to make sure that only people who are serious about using it actually sign up. If you think about the way your feature works now, that will give you clues as to what the company's objectives are.

I'll close here with a quick example. I might select Google Maps and explain that I like:

- The fact that you can download offline maps to conserve data from your phone plan
- The way that it integrates with my Google Calendar to automatically suggest places that it knows I'll be going to soon
- The ability to select a certain time of departure when I'm getting directions, so I know what traffic will look like then

I would improve it by integrating with airline data to suggest flights as a mode of transportation if you ask it to give you directions between two places that are distant from one another.

When asked why they haven't done this already, I would say that they already have a product for flight search (Google Flights). While it might be convenient for some people to use Google Maps to plan trips, it doesn't make sense to invest the effort to add that feature, since it would likely just cannibalize customers from another Google product anyway. People also generally look for flights using flight search engines, so it would likely take some time for people to get used to searching from a different interface (and people might not want to use a new interface for this at all). Given those issues, it would not make sense to expend resources on building this.

What does a product manager do?

I really like this question when I'm interviewing candidates, if only because it offers a great reminder of how ambiguous the role of product manager actually is. If you ask this to 100 candidates, you'll get 100 different answers (and most of them will be right). When my grandparents ask what I do, I explain to them that I tell the developers what to build. The reality, though, is that only covers the most basic part of product management.

The product manager is a leader but not a people manager, a resource for employees and customers alike, and an important decision maker who guides not only the product but the company. It is a role that changes significantly depending on the context, and that's why it's always interesting to hear other PMs answer this question.

I have a stock answer to this that I won't share here - if you just want to borrow someone else's answer, you can find plenty online with a quick Googling. Instead, here's a quick exercise to come up with your own.

Consider this - if all the product managers suddenly disappeared from your company, what work would stop getting done (at least until someone else takes over)? Because the role of the PM is so abstract and varied, this can be a helpful way to think about it concretely. No one will be planning sprints, that's for sure. But what else? In the past I've trained sales teams on my products before they launch, but at a lot of organizations there are sales enablement folks to do that. I've helped write marketing copy when that team was really busy. When I'm running beta programs for new products, I'm effectively customer support for those programs.

Those experiences reflect the fact that I've been at early-stage startups - if you're at Facebook, Google, Salesforce or any other giant tech company, there are plenty of marketing folks, and it's unlikely you'd need to fill in there. They also reflect my history working in enterprise software - consumer PMs likely haven't spent time training sales teams.

The point here isn't to get the correct answer, but rather to offer some insight into your history and experience. One more specific piece of advice that I will offer, though, is to tell the interviewer that the product manager is the person ultimately responsible for the success or failure of his product. Whatever type of company you're working at, that will always be the case, and it shows that you understand not just what a PM does, but also the importance of the role.

After you've answered, you should turn it around and ask your interviewer how your answer lines up with the work that PMs do at her company. If your answer was spot on, great. If there are differences between what you described and what PMs do there, it's helpful to find them out, so that you can address them and give the interviewer confidence that you'll be able to handle the role.

Why do you want to work here?

This interview question is in no way unique to product managers, but it's particularly important. It's something of a running joke that when this question gets asked at minimum-wage jobs like working at a fast food restaurant, it's ridiculous, because the answer is obvious - for the paycheck. Nobody's working as a fry cook at McDonald's because of a deep-seated passion for frying potato slivers all day.

For a product manager, it's a much more valid (and important) question. A PM sits at the center of the company, influencing not only product but culture. Especially for early stage startups, though certainly still at more established companies, hiring a product manager who doesn't care about the company and is just there to collect a paycheck can negatively impact the morale of lots of people. Many employees will view product managers as leaders (rightfully so), and when you see leaders doing the minimum and clocking out as soon as the clock strikes five, it's not particularly inspiring.

The most obvious way to approach this question is to talk about the company's product. Ideally, you're interviewing at a company that makes something or provides a service that you're deeply passionate about. If you have a deep connection to what the company is doing, this is the time to let them know.

This might be because of personal experience. I interviewed at a startup that's bringing technology to the home care industry while my very elderly grandmother needed full-time help, and that gave me a window into just how fragmented and disorganized that industry is. When I think about the service they're providing and the people they're providing it to, who are some of the most vulnerable out there, it certainly makes me think that applying technology to provide transparency and accountability is a really, really valuable thing. That sort of experience is a great reason to want to join a company, because it shows them you really care about what they're doing and will bring that passion to work.

You may also have experience with the problem they're trying to solve. I invest in real estate on the side, and from that experience I know that the process of buying real estate is absolutely awful and that the technology tools available to landlords, property managers and investors are not great. When I interview at real estate tech startups, this is a big plus for them, because I bring the same experiences their target customers will have had, along with a personal desire to fix what I recognize are significant problems.

But what if you don't have a passion for what the company is doing? When I reflect on the jobs I've worked at and the products they've built - cloud content management, enterprise video conferencing, call center software - it's very clear that I didn't get into those jobs because I cared deeply about the problems they were solving. That's okay, because there are plenty of other reasons to join a company.

For me, the two most important things I'm looking for are company culture and impact. Having worked on rather unglamorous software, I can say that just because you aren't working on the next photo-sharing app doesn't mean the product isn't interesting. In fact, some of the least sexy problems are some of the most complex and intellectually stimulating to work on.

With that in mind, if I'm interviewing at an early-stage startup, I'll tell the interviewer that I have found in my experience that companies at their stage tend to have the kind of culture I'm looking for. People don't join a 50 person company just for the paycheck, and so you tend to get the kind of people who are doers and problems solvers. On top of that, being one of the first PMs allows you to have a lot of impact not just on your area of the product, but also on the internal processes of the company and the culture. These are things that greatly appeal to me, and they're also the sort of things that hiring managers (hopefully) want in someone they're bringing on board.

On the other hand, when I've interviewed at larger companies, I've been able to highlight the appeal that they have to me as well. While I won't have as big of an impact on the company culture, I'll be working on products that serve a large number of people, which is impactful in a different way. I'll also have access to the kinds of resources and experienced leadership that are often not present in small companies.

As you think about this question, consider all of the things that are important to you, not just the product you might be working on. I also encourage you to give an honest answer - don't tell the hiring manager at a startup focused on improving trash pickup that you have a deep passion for waste management if you don't. Remember, interviews are a two-way street. You're trying to show how you're a good fit for the job, but you should also be trying to evaluate if the company is a good fit for you. If they're willing to reject you because you don't wake up in the morning and go to sleep at night thinking about how exciting their product is, it's probably not going to be a great place for you to work.

PM INTERVIEW QUESTIONS - DESIGN

As I mentioned in the previous chapter, experience questions are one of two main types that you'll get when you interview for product management jobs. The other type is design questions. These include all the hypothetical questions you'll get about products - some will ask you to design a new product for a particular use case, while others will ask you to critique an existing product. I'm also including case-type questions in this section, as some product managers prefer them to more traditional design questions.

Before we get to the actual questions, a few tips. First, understand and manage your time. The amount of time you have for a particular question is a clue to the level of depth the interviewer is looking for in your answers. Some interviewers will dedicate most of the time they have with you to a single design question - in this case, you should be getting deep into the specifics, probably down to the user story level. On the other hand, some interviewers will throw several design questions at you, in addition to some about your experience. If that happens, it's generally best to focus on the approach that you would take to the design problem without going too deep into the actual specific features. It never hurts to ask about this - if an interviewer starts with a product design question, you can always explain that you want to manage your time correctly, so you'd like to know how many design questions you're going to be answering.

While you should manage your time, I also strongly advise you not to rush. Take a few minutes to think through things before you start diving into the problem. The framework below is designed to help with that, so try to do a quick runthrough of it in your head once you hear the question. You don't need to have your entire answer carefully plotted out before you write anything on the whiteboard, but remember that you're being judged not just on your answer to the question, but also on how clear and well-organized your communication is. Taking two or three minutes to think through your answer is time well spent if it means that you can communicate your thoughts in a well-structured way.

As you spend a few minutes thinking through the question, ask clarifying questions. There are more details about the kinds of questions you should be asking below, but I want to emphasize that you're expected to ask questions and that the interviewer is evaluating your ability to ask good ones. The vast majority of design questions have purposefully omitted important information, and part of your job is to figure out what that is. Again, this is where a framework really comes in handy - if you have a big, general picture of what's expected out of a design question, it makes it much easier to figure out where there are missing pieces that need to be filled in before you can give a good answer.

Lastly, don't be nervous! I recognize that if you could cure your nerves magically because someone told you to, you probably would have done so already, so let me be more specific. Remember that if you're being interviewed, the company wants to hire you. They created an open position because there's work that needs to be done, and that means that work is either not being done right now, or its being done by somebody who is overworked (if so, that person is almost always going to be on the interview panel). If they don't hire you, they're stuck in that state until they find someone to hire. Also, interviewing is expensive! Taking up hours of collective time from product managers, engineers and executives to interview a product candidate is a big commitment by the company - these are highly compensated folks we're talking about. If every interview takes five hours of time, that's five hours of time not spent making a better product. If they decline to give you an offer, that means at least five more hours lost interviewing the next candidate, and nobody wants that. So trust me when I say that the panel is on your side, even if their poker faces don't show it.

With that in mind, let's take a look at a framework that we can use to answer the majority of these questions.

Question Framework

Design questions can be challenging, as they give you a lot of leeway and purposely incomplete information. They don't just test your ability to design a product, but also your ability to gather the relevant information so that you can make the right decision.

For that reason, and in order to have a clear, organized answer, it's important that you come in with a framework in mind to tackle each part of the question in an orderly fashion. For design questions, I like to go through four steps:

1. Objectives
2. Users
3. Constraints
4. Features

The first three are really about gathering information, while the last step is when you'll get into design.

One important note before you get started is to use the whiteboard if there is one. As you hear the question, write down the important parts. When you go through each of the steps I've listed below, write things down. Using the board saves you from having to keep details in your mind, and it also gives the interviewer a visual way to see you move through the problem.

Objectives

Design questions will often be phrased in such a way that you're told what to design, but generally not why. Without knowing the objective, though, you can't possibly come up with a good design. What if, for example, someone told you to design a building. If all you know is that it needs to be a building, you can't possibly do a good job. Is it a home for someone to live in? An apartment building for many people to live in? An office building? A medical facility?

Make sure that you're 100% clear on the objective before you move on - if I have a whiteboard, I like to write this at the top and double check with the interviewer that they agree about what the objective is.

Users

You may know what you need to build and why you're building it, but without knowing who you're building it for, you have plenty of room to make significant mistakes. Going back to the building example, let's say you're told that you need to build a single family home for a family of four.

You decide you need three bedrooms, two baths, a yard for the kids and a few other rooms. Unfortunately, you failed to include the wheelchair ramp that the family's disabled son needs to get in and out of the house. That's because you didn't ask about the people who are going to be living in the house. You absolutely must know who your users are before you can design a product (and I mean that for both interview questions and the actual job of being a product manager).

Constraints

The users may have certain constraints that come along with them, but there will likely be other constraints you need to find in the problem as well. Putting in arbitrary restrictions on what you are allowed to do helps the interviewer make sure that you're thinking on your feet, plus it's a good way to make sure you're asking enough questions.

Now that you know you need to build a house for a family with a disabled child, find out what else you might need to know to get the design right. Does the house need to be in a specific location that might affect it? A beach house may have different requirements than one in snow country. Does it need to be made of a specific material? Do you have a particular budget? Are there any restrictions on size? Do you have a certain amount of time to build it?

As you listen to the problem, think about what goes into building the product you're asked to design and what things the interviewer can limit to make it more challenging. Consider time, resources, materials, the process for building it and the people/machines that will need to build it. The sample questions below have examples of the kinds of constraints that an interviewer might use.

Features

Once you have the background provided by finding the objectives, users and constraints, it's time to start actually designing the product. The best place to start is with a list of what it actually needs to do.

Make sure that you do this in an organized fashion. I like to walk through the process of using a product from start to finish in order to ensure that I get everything. With a house, for example, if I were coming home from work, I would enter first (so I need a front door and an entryway). After that I would set my stuff down in my office, then go to the bathroom. I'd cook some dinner, which would need a kitchen, then I'd eat it, so a dining room is necessary. I would watch some TV after dinner in the living room, then I'd go to bed in the bedroom. You don't have to use that particular method, just make sure you have an orderly system to go through the features, so that you sound organized and don't miss anything.

Design a vending machine/train ticket sale kiosk/ride-sharing

app/something else for the blind.

There are plenty of other variations beyond the ones listed, but you get the idea - the interviewer wants to take a product that you're familiar with, introduce a new constraint (the user is blind) and see if you can come up with a new version of that product that's usable given the constraint.

Let's go through the four steps and come up with a conclusion.

Objective

As with all design questions, you'll want to start with the objective - what is it that we hope this vending machine (I'll use that version of the question for the rest of this analysis) is going to achieve? This sounds straightforward - they said in the question that it's a vending machine for the blind, so the objective is to sell goods to blind people. That's not the objective, though; it's just a feature. The objective isn't what it needs to do, but why.

So why are creating this vending machine? Is it because the blind are an underserved market, and our goal is to make as much profit as possible? Is it to provide a service to blind people with no need for profit? If you don't get to the real objective, you may start designing a vending machine that sells chips and soda to the blind when the real goal was to design a vending machine that gives out free audio headsets that give guided tours in a museum for the blind.

Users

If you think we can skip past this step because we know the users are blind people, think again. The question didn't state whether *only* blind people can use the machine, and that's critical to clarify. If you assume it's for blind people only, but it turns out it needs to be usable for everyone, you're going to make the design mistake of not including an interface for sighted people. If the objective of your vending machine is profit, but most of the population can't use it, you've done a poor job of designing it.

Even if it's the museum use case, distributing headsets for the blind, you might still want an interface for sighted people. What if a group of children from a school for the blind come, and some of their chaperones are sighted? They might need to be able to use the vending machine to get headsets for all the kids.

Remember that you can get to some of these answers without asking specifically about every person who might use it. A broad question like, "Are there any reasons that sighted people might need to use the machine?" can help the interviewer guide you what he has in mind. He might not tell you exactly what use cases you need to handle for sighted people, but even a response of "Well, what do you think?" means that it's something you should spend time considering.

There is also one other user to consider - the person who has to stock the vending machine. Don't forget this person, or you'll end up with a vending machine that needs to be replaced every time it gets emptied out.

Constraints

Think through the constraints that a vending machine has to see where you're limited in your design. Location may be one - are these vending machines going to be in a loud, crowded venue like a high school or an airport, or are they going to be in a quiet, controlled environment? On a similar note, consider the type of people that are going to be at the location where the vending machine is. If it's a high school and you design your vending machine with a high-end touchscreen LED interface, you're going to lose money when teenagers keep breaking it. Instead, you need to seriously consider durability.

Consider what it takes to keep a vending machine running - as mentioned above, it needs to be stocked and may require maintenance. It's likely the maintenance people will be sighted, so you need to take this into account and ensure they have a way to interact with the machine.

In this example, construction constraints don't usually come up (e.g. constraints around who is building it, how quickly it needs to be build, what it's build of), but if you're not sure whether they're relevant, it never hurts to ask.

Features

As we start to design the vending machine, let's assume that it's a traditional chips and soda vending machine, and it's going to be placed in malls throughout the country. The goal is to make as much money as possible, but because we're receiving a grant from a charity that helps the blind, it's equally important that it be fully usable by blind people. The mall maintenance staff will be responsible for maintaining and restocking the machines.

WIth that in mind, let's walk through the steps of using a vending machine to figure out everything we need to include to have a successful product.

First, we need to locate the vending machine. This is a step that a lot of people forget when answering this question. Instead, they start after the blind person is beginning to interact with the machine. This is a serious omission, because making the machine locatable is a hugely important design consideration. As a sighted person, I just see vending machines as I'm walking around; this is obviously not the case for the blind.

Since we don't have sight to work with, we'll have to figure out how a blind person can locate a machine by sound, touch, taste or smell. Taste and smell aren't going to be especially useful here, so that leaves us sound and touch. One easy way to let blind people locate the machine is just to put a very large siren on the top that plays a loud noise constantly. Unfortunately, that wouldn't go over well with mall owners, since it would annoy people into leaving the mall. Thus, we need to find a solution that works for blind people without being obnoxious for everyone.

When I'm asked this question, I always ask the interviewer clarifying questions about how blind people interact in the world. Consider the things that you do frequently that blind people must need to do in a mall - find a bathroom, locate a particular store, pay for and pick up food at the food court. I've gotten different answers to these questions from different interviewers, but that's fine - take the relevant parts of their answers and try to adapt those to the vending machine use case.

One example of a response I've gotten is that there are standard rules around the placement of signage and information in a mall - it's why every bathroom door you see has the same men/women's icons located in the same place on the bathroom door with braille in the same location relative to the sign. Since that means there is already a system in place to find specific locations that blind people are familiar with, you should just add the vending machine to that system.

In another version of this question that I've received, one of the conditions given was that half the world has become blind. In this case, I considered what the world would be like and figured that there would probably be a mass-market device designed specifically for blind people - likely a modified iPhone or similar product. It would certainly have functionality to help locate places (perhaps maps that are searchable and give directions via voice on a headset, and the option to have the phone vibrate when you're close to your location), so we should just use that to help people find the vending machine. If you're going to make assumptions about the world like this, be sure to state them clearly and check that your interviewer finds them reasonable.

The next step after locating the vending machine is to determine what's in it, so I can figure out what I want. There are a couple of ways I see to do this for a blind person - sound and touch. Since one of our constraints is that we're in a mall, audio can be tough, as it's likely loud with poor acoustics. If the user can plug in a headset, that solves the loudness issue, but we probably can't assume that every blind person will have a headset (though as with all assumptions, you should check this with the interviewer).

So with that in mind, let's focus on touch. We can create a braille menu of items in the machine along with their prices, but the items can change over time. That means we need a surface that can display braille but be updated based on inputs from the maintenance crew. The surface also needs to have buttons on or next to it to allow for selection of items from the menu, and it also needs to be able to display words for sighted people. Beyond that, we should also have some braille instructions on how to use the machine in a place that's easy to locate - since those won't change over time, they can just be static.

After I choose what I want from the menu, I need to pay for it - we can handle this via a standard credit card reader and a place to put in bills and coins plus dispense change.

Once I've paid, I should get the item I've selected. Again, this can be handled in standard vending machine fashion, with a slot at the bottom where items are dispensed.

That covers the whole end user experience, but as we touched on earlier, there's another user - the maintenance person responsible for stocking the machine. We can gloss over some of the details of restocking the machine, since most of them aren't specific to the blind person use case and thus aren't interesting for this problem.

That said, since the items in the machine may change, we need the maintenance person to have an interface inside the machine to input the menu options. I would just put in a simple keyboard and small screen to select a vending machine slot and type in the item that's in it. You can go further with this (consider that maintenance people may not be native English speakers, thus you don't want them typing things in and a bar code scanner may be better), but check with your interviewer before you get too deep. This isn't a core piece of the exercise, and for time-related reasons they'll likely want to stop after you've addressed the end-user use case.

Now that you've talked through everything you need, make sure you clearly summarize at the end. Because this is a very visual problem, I highly recommend drawing a visual representation of your vending machine. I've included a drawing from me below - as you'll see, it's very low quality, but that's fine because it has the appropriate level of detail for the problem.

"To summarize, we need a way for a user to locate the vending machine, which we'll achieve by integrating it into all of the other signage and direction mechanisms for the blind that already exist within malls. We need a way to for people to know what's in the machine. Sighted people can see the options, while blind people will have a braille interface that can be updated as the menu changes, along with static braille instructions on where to find the interface and how to use the machine. We need a way to pay for items, receive change and receive the items - these will all be handled by standard vending machine interfaces for these purposes. Lastly, we will need a way for the maintenance workers to update menu items and prices as they change stock, which will be handled by a keyboard and computer screen inside the machine."

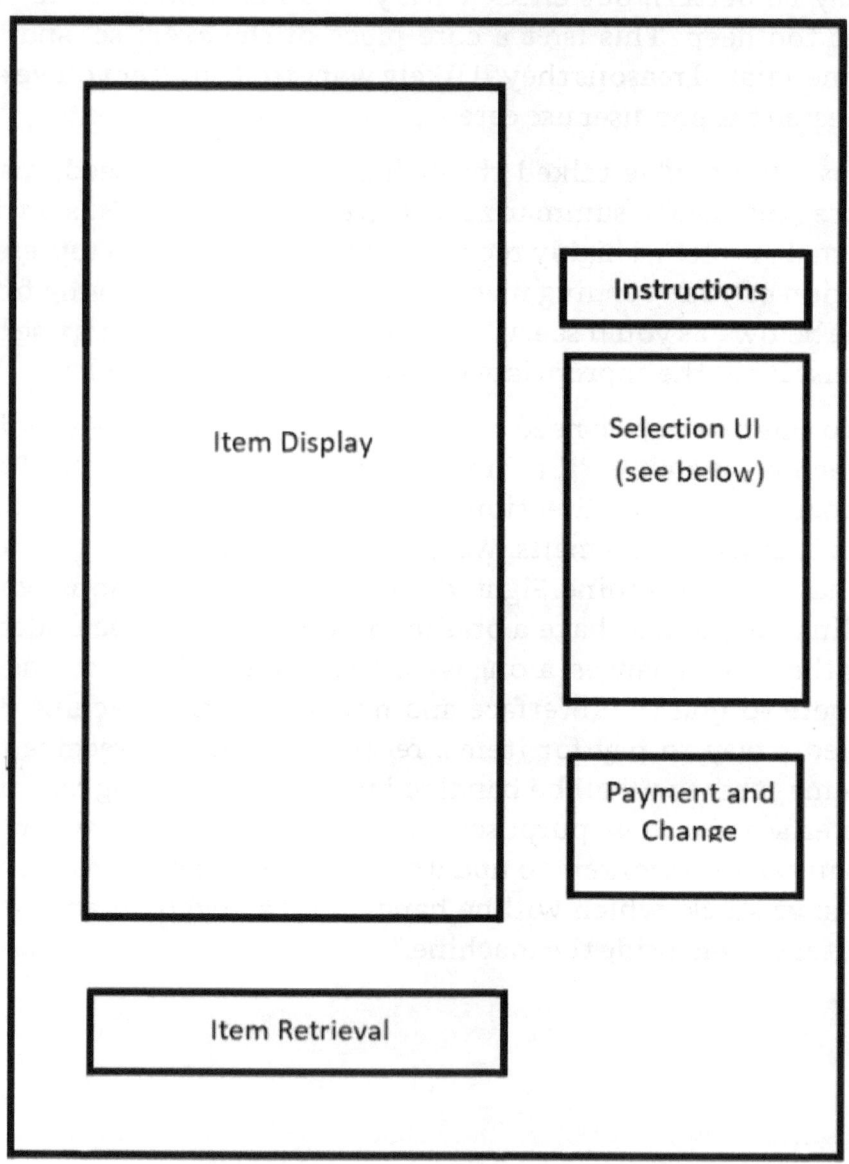

The Product Management Interview

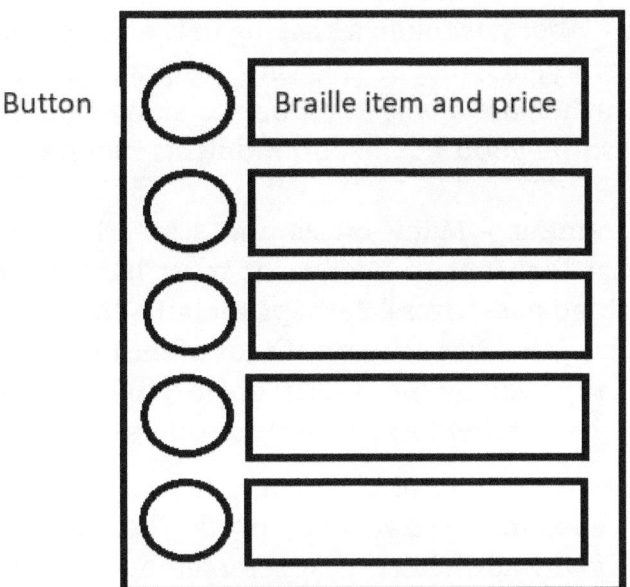

Create <tool> for <user>.

There are a million variations of this, and interviewers often like to come up with their own. I've been asked to help design audio equipment for a looper (naturally my first question was what a looper is - I'll let you Google that one), a pen for an astronaut and a UI for my grandma to use Uber even though she won't use a smartphone.

Regardless, the same basic structure applies - get all of your relevant background information, then step through the features you'll need in an organized fashion.

For this example, let's go with a UI for my grandma (or other, similar elderly people) to use Uber.

Objective

We need to create a way for elderly people without smartphones to use Uber, but why? There are a few possible goals:

- Maximize profit - This is a set of users not served by the ridesharing market that might be potentially lucra-

tive, since many of them are unable to drive.
- Public service - Uber has taken a beating in the press over the last couple of years; maybe this isn't designed to drive revenue, but rather it's a way for Uber to show that it's helping to do some good in the communities in which it operates.
- Legal requirement - Many cities and states have requirements that for Uber to operate, it must have a way to handle disabled passengers. Perhaps socially-conscious cities, seeing that Uber has driven out a lot of the taxis that were traditionally used by the elderly, are forcing it to find a way to serve them if it wants to continue operating.

Each of these objectives will drive different conclusions about product design. If we're aiming to generate profit, then we have to consider carefully any additional costs created by our solution here - if we're doing it to generate good PR around the service we're providing, then cost is much less important. If we're doing it for legal reasons, we will probably need to provide some kind of reporting to cities/states to show that we're in compliance with their regulations.

Users

We know one set of users is going to be elderly people without smartphones. We should also consider people who help take care of the elderly, like family members and caretakers. Those people will likely have smartphones and may want to be able to use those to call rides for the elderly from the Uber app, but let the driver know it's an elderly person who may need help getting in/out, etc. They may also want tools to help the elderly person manage the payment side of things and view receipts for previous trips.

The drivers are also users here. If we expect them to behave differently with elderly people (e.g. going to the door and ringing the bell instead of just waiting for them to come out), they'll need to be trained on how to handle these cases and notified when they're being hailed by an elderly person.

Constraints

The big constraint is in the question - no smartphone. What other constraints might an elderly person have, though. Do they have email to receive receipts and other information? My grandma doesn't trust any internet service with her credit card - do we need to allow them to pay via other methods?

Features

Let's make the following assumptions as we figure out our product features:

- The goal is public service. We're trying to do something good for the community, so profit isn't the primary driver (though we still can't bankrupt the company).
- The core users here are going to be elderly people without smartphones.
- Since these people will likely require significant help from family/caregivers, we should also address their needs in our solution (but we can also count on their help for some of the account setup and management functionality).
- Same with drivers - we should consider anything required for them to provide a good service.
- We will only take credit cards as a payment option.
- We cannot rely on our elderly customers to use email.

With those in mind, let's walk through the process of taking an Uber ride and consider what we need to do to allow an elderly person without a smartphone to take one.

Before we can take a ride at all, we need to set up an Uber account. That means downloading the app, entering an email and password to create an account and putting in credit card information.

After that, when I want to take a ride, I open up the app, input my current location and destination, select which type of Uber

I want to take (e.g. UberX, UberBLACK, UberPOOL, etc.) and then press okay and confirm the fare. I am then notified when a car is headed my way, and I can see its location on the map. I am notified again when it is close. I am also notified if the driver cancels the ride.

Once the car is at my pickup location, I have to correctly identify it and get in. When I get to my destination, I get out, and the app automatically charges my credit card and generates a receipt that I can find in the app. I have the option to rate the driver and provide feedback.

Looking at that list, it's clear that a lot of functionality requires the Uber app, so we have a lot to take care of. Let's break it down in a logical fashion and take it piece by piece. First let's look at account set up.

We can't use a smartphone, so let's look at the other options we have available to us. We can assume elderly customers will have landline phones, as well as access to the mail. We also stated earlier that we can assume that family and caregivers can help out. This seems like a good place to involve them. Since we can safely assume they'll have access to the internet, let's create a special website for people to register Uber accounts for elderly people. Depending on how much money we're willing to spend on this program, we might also have people who can go to elderly people's houses to them sign up or a phone line they can call where an Uber employee can sign up for them.

The current requirements to create an account are email, password and payment information. We can't rely on the elderly to have email, so we should substitute phone number for email.

Once we've created an account, our users need a way to call an Uber. Let's again rely on phone here - give them a phone number that they can call to get a ride. We could make this an automated telephone system or actually have a person answer. The latter seems like a better fit, as an elderly person may have trouble interacting with an automated phone system. Paying people to answer the phone is more expensive, but that's okay, since we've stated that cost is not a primary factor here.

The person answering the phone needs to know the user's pickup and dropoff locations. Consider the places our elderly person might go - to run errands, to visit family, to go to the doctor. She may not remember the addresses for all of these things, and she's likely particuar about the places she wants to go (when she wants to get groceries, she's going to want to go to the market that she's used to). She's probably also usually going to the same few places. Given this, I think we can improve the experience here by getting a list of locations during account setup - home, relatives' addresses, favorite stores and doctor's office (plus any other common locations). We'll revisit how we collect that info a bit later, but for now let's assume that the user will have a basic list of places she can visit, which she can tell to the person answering the phone.

Next, she needs to pick what type of Uber she wants. This could get confusing, as there are a lot of choices, and it would be a pain to explain them to an elderly person over the phone. We can simplify this by assuming that all riders want to take UberX (which I choose because it's relatively low cost but also doesn't come with the extra complication of sharing a ride with others). The big exception is people who are disabled and need a special vehicle - we should also add that to the list of info we collect during account setup. Some wealthier customers might also want a black car instead of UberX.

Once the car arrives, she's going to need to be notified that it's there. The best way to do this is to train the driver to walk to the house or apartment and ring the bell or knock on the door (since this will also allow him to help her to the car if necessary). The driver will need to know that this is necessary, since it's not usually the case for passengers, so we'll need to add something to the Uber driver app to clarify this.

When she arrives at the destination, her driver will let her know and help her out of the car. Her payment will be automatically charged to the credit card. We can put a receipt into the admin interface that her caretaker users, but we may also need to mail one, since we can't count on her having email or access to that admin portal.

To summarize, we'll need to create or modify four components:

- Create a portal for a caretaker or family member to set up an Uber account on behalf of an elderly person
- Create a phone service that the elderly person can call to request a ride
- Modify the driver app to let drivers know when they have an elderly passenger who needs them to come to the door
- Create a service that mails receipts when necessary

Now let's go into the specifics of each of those services.

Web Portal

The web portal should have a few pieces of functionality:

- A user must be able to create an account by entering name, phone and password, as well as payment information
- A user must be able to view and edit personal and payment info
- A user must be able to view ride history and receipts
- A user on the portal must be able to create, delete and update travel locations
- A user on the portal must be able to specify what car type is needed for rides (UberX, UberBLACK or a disabled vehicle)
- A user on the portal should be able to delete the account
- A user should be able to add any special instructions for the driver about pickup and dropoff (i.e. enter a door or gate code)
- A user should be able to choose if the elderly person receives receipts by mail or only in the portal

Phone Service

The phone service will need a few things:

- Phone agents should be able to identify the caller based on their phone number and pull up their account information
- Phone agents must be able to book rides on behalf of customers to and from their pre-set destinations
- Phone agents must be able to see the price of the ride as well as which car is assigned to it and approximate wait time

Driver App

The driver app must be updated to give a clear notification to drivers that they are picking up an elderly passenger and will need to go to the door, along with any notes entered about pickup details.

Mail Service

The mail service should automatically mail a receipt with ride information and cost details to customers who have chosen to receive receipts via mail.

That covers the functionality, but there are a lot of follow up questions an interviewer can ask. We haven't addressed how an elderly person might get back from the place they're dropped off. There are ways to address this - for example, pre-scheduled return rides or partnerships with common destinations like doctors' offices that allow them to schedule rides back on behalf of patients.

You may also get questions about safety and security - what happens if something goes wrong (perhaps the web portal should have emergency contact info and other instructions of what to do in an emergency)? What if drivers cancel rides for older people because they always take extra time? You could easily ban those drivers from the platform, but it's not really fair to make less money on their rides because of the passengers you send them. Given that, maybe they should be more highly compensated for these rides.

There are lots of details to dive into, so as you're asked follow up questions, just make sure you're getting clarification and addressing them in an organized way, as you have with the rest of the question.

Have you used our product? What works well about it, and what needs improvement?

This is a little different than other product design questions, but I'm finishing the section with it because it's fundamentally a question of understanding and assessing the design of products. It's important to note that this is one question where you should not be using the general framework for design questions. This one isn't about your process, it's about your opinions, but even more than that it's about your preparedness.

The interviewer isn't expecting you to have a thorough, in-depth critique of the product, but she is expecting that you've tried it and thought about it. Product managers tend to look at all products in the world with a critical eye, so if you've spent some time with a product, you ought to have some thoughts on how it could be improved.

Your answer to the first part of this question needs to be yes. When I'm an interviewer, if you come onsite and haven't bothered to check out my product yet, I'm going to vote against hiring you. The exception is if you have a fantastic reason for not having tried it or have otherwise completely blown me away with your qualifications. Also, there are some cases where it's not possible to try a product, especially when it comes to fairly complex enterprise software that requires significant configuration. If that's the case, when I'm a candidate, I still like to ask the recruiter if there is a demo account I can try out or if someone can demo the product during my interviews - after all, I want to have at least a decent understanding of the product I'm going to be working on if I'm hired.

The reality is that if you're looking to join a company as a product manager, you should really want to understand their product. If you haven't done the absolute most basic research possible, it's tough for me to believe that you really want the job or that you can be trusted to be thorough and reliable in research you'll have to do if you get hired.

Before you come in for an interview at any company, give their product a try. Take notes while you're doing it on what's good and what's bad. You don't have to go especially deep or try everything, but you should have a few meaningful criticisms ready to go. Don't worry about offending the interviewer - any good product manager can take critiques of his products. In fact, most PMs tend to be the harshest critics of their products, so it's unlikely you'll shock them with your critiques.

PM INTERVIEW QUESTIONS - PROBLEM SOLVING

As a PM, you won't just be constantly building products from scratch. A significant, though less glamorous, part of the job is diagnosing and resolving issues that arise with your products.

Some of these will be bugs and technical issues - as a PM, you're the expert on all of your products, which means tricky issues that support can't solve will get escalated to you. It's important that you be able to evaluate and diagnose most confusing issues that arise. The alternative is just to file bugs and send them off to your engineering team, but every time you do that, you sacrifice engineering time that could be better used elsewhere.

One of the most direct ways you can impact your engineering team's ability to produce features is to resolve issues yourself. Even if you can't resolve them, you should be able to handle much of the investigation - determining the cause of a problem still saves your engineering team time, since they can move right into fixing it.

For that reason, many interviewers will ask you hypothetical questions about how you would handle issues (or things that appear to be issues). As with other questions we've discussed, the goal here is to understand your process - it's not necessarily that you should be able to diagnose the cause of a hypothetical problem, but you should approach it in a structured, methodical way.

Besides resolving issues that have arisen, questions of this type can also be about improvements - how do you solve the problem of leads converting to paid accounts at a low rate, or how do you drive more usage of a newly launched feature? These are often called funnel optimization problems, and they're core to the work of many PMs, especially those working on consumer-facing products..

Framework

The most important thing to bear in mind when approaching all of these questions is that it's critical to use data. Step one is to understand the issue, and that will always require looking at the numbers to understand what is currently happening and who it is currently happening to. When dealing with bugs, knowing who is affected will allow you to narrow down the causes - a bug affecting all users of one specific part of your product should be treated very differently than a bug affecting a specific subset of users that are unable to use your whole product.

For funnel optimization questions, the data will tell you what is happening right now, so you have a starting point to figure out what changes to make. If you're trying to improve usage of a new feature, it matters whether people just aren't aware of that feature, or whether they start to use it and then stop before they're done. Use the data to answer those questions before you go any further.

There are really only three basic steps to a problem solving type of question:

1. Validate the problem
2. Diagnose the problem
3. Prioritize the solution to the problem

You can often skip the first step - if the interviewer says there's a specific problem, you can take him at his word that it exists. In some cases, though, you're just going to get a more high level description of a behavior change or a situation, and in those cases you'll need to validate that a problem actually exists, and that there isn't a reasonable explanation for what you're seeing.

Some interviewers won't even care about the third step, so if they cut you off when you start getting into the details of how urgent it is to fix something, don't worry about it. The reality is that the diagnosis alone is a good way of testing some of your general product management skills - regardless of what problem is thrown at you, you should be able to approach it in a methodical way. Finding an actual solution often depends much more on domain expertise than soft skills, so if you have significant domain expertise, this is a good time to demonstrate it. If not, a good interviewer should have limited expectations of your ability to suggest creative solutions.

You're the product manager for all of a consumer company's mobile products. Yesterday, your number of daily active mobile users was down 20% from the day before. What do you do?

This is a pretty common question with plenty of variants - usage has dropped, so figure out why. The details of the question are usually a clue to the issue, so keep them in mind. I'll explain later in this answer why the fact that this is mobile matters.

First, let's validate the problem - we've seen a 20% drop in daily active users, but that's just an observation. It seems like a problem, but there are reasons you might see a 20% drop in users that are totally reasonable and expected. Perhaps you're dealing with a seasonal product; it would make perfect sense that an app built to count down the days until Christmas sees a huge drop in users on December 26 (in fact if it only saw a 20% drop, I'd be shocked).

Also, in this case, all you know is that usage dropped from one day to the next, but it's tough to know if that's a problem without seeing the bigger picture. What if usage was much higher than usual yesterday because of a promotion the company ran? In that case, a drop of 20% might just be an expected return to regular usage levels and not an issue at all.

To validate that we do in fact have a problem, then, I'm going to first try to figure out if there's an explicable cause for the change that does not indicate an issue. First, if I don't know exactly what the product I'm managing is, I'm going to find that out. If the interviewer says that I'm a PM on Facebook's core product, then I can rule out a non-problematic explanation for a 20% swing - there's no reason that should happen.

Next, I'll tell the interviewer that I would first look at usage over the past 30 days, as well as daily usage from the same month last year. This will tell me if this change in users is explained by a larger pattern in the data. If the interviewer just tells you that the data was going up steadily until yesterday or draws a crude graph showing that, then you've got your answer - this is a real problem. If he says this is a decline from a marketing-driven spike in usage yesterday, then you have your answer as well.

Let's assume that this 20% drop is an anomaly, since that will usually be the case in an interview. We've now validated the problem, so next we need to diagnose it. We'll start doing that by looking into the data.

In a question like this, there will really be two reasons that usage would have dropped. You're either dealing with a *behavioral change* or a *technical issue*. The former just means that people have actually stopped using the app - they made a decision not to do so yesterday, for some reason that you need to figure out. Alternatively, you may be dealing with a technical issue - people were trying to use the app as normal but had issues that prevented them from doing so.

To figure out which it is, we need to figure out who stopped using the app. We know 20% fewer people accessed the app, but we need to dig into the data to determine who those people are. To do that, I'm going to start looking at subsets of my user base to see how they were affected relatively to the overall 20%

drop.

Since I'm dealing with mobile, first I'm going to break down the mobile user base into small categories, and the logical first step there is device. I'll ask the interviewer if there is a difference in usage between Android and iOS. I'll also go more granular than that - both Android and iOS work on different devices, and there are different versions of each operating system out there, so I'm going to break down the data along those lines and see how usage looks for each subgroup.

Let's say the interviewer tells me that iOS users showed no drop in usage, but Android showed a 40% drop. All subgroups of Android users showed roughly the same percentage decline. Now we know it's an issue with Android users, but we still can't be sure whether it's a technical issue or a behavioral one.

I'm now going to start breaking down my Android user base into demographic categories to see whether there is any difference in usage along those lines. I'll ask the interviewer a series of questions about basic demographics: how does the drop in usage yesterday look in men vs. women, in different age groups, and in different places?

Let's say the interviewer tells me there was no difference based on gender or age, but there's a huge one in location - it looks like almost the entire drop in usage came from China. In fact, there was virtually no usage in China whatsoever yesterday.

At this point, you have a good enough idea of who is affected to start figuring out what the problem is, though in this case you may have guessed already - Facebook was blocked in China yesterday. You won't need to go further here, since the mobile PM definitely isn't going to be tasked with negotiating with the Chinese government to get Facebook unblocked. That's fine, because you've shown that were able to use data to narrow down the source of the problem.

It's worth noting that Android was a big clue - if something goes wrong there, it's likely an international issue, since Android phones are so much more prevalent outside the United States than in it. This was actually a real question that was asked of me, and I missed that clue. That wasn't a problem, though, since I got to the right answer anyway and the interviewer knew I didn't have a background as a mobile PM. If you have focused on mobile in the past, though, that would have been a good opportunity to demonstrate some of your domain expertise.

There are endless variations on this question, but the approach is generally the same - look at the data to try to understand the problem better. Once you know what's happening, you can prioritize it like any other bug.

A customer service rep comes to you and says that there's a significant bug with one of your products that has just arisen and needs to be resolved ASAP. What do you do?

Again, there are many variations here, but the point here is to figure out how you deal with bugs. We'll use the same three step process I described above.

Validate the Problem

Before you start filing bugs or alerting engineering, you should make sure that the problem actually exists. Especially when this question is asked with a customer service rep bringing the problem to your attention (as opposed to someone more technical like an engineer, for example), I like to point out that people often make too many assumptions when reporting bugs to a product manager.

What I mean by that is that people often see a symptom, but they make assumptions about the cause of that symptom and just report that assumed cause to you. For example, a support rep might come to you and tell you that your product's email alerts are broken, because several customers have reported not receiving email alerts when they should have. The rep doesn't know the email alert system is broken, he just knows the symptoms - emails not appearing when expected - and assumes the cause. The reality might be that your email alerts are going out fine but Gmail has decided that they're spam, so Gmail users aren't seeing them.

Thus, the first thing you should do when a customer support rep tells you there's a problem is to ask what they think the problem is and why they think that. The goal here is to get past any analysis they've done - for now, you don't want analysis; you just want to know exactly what problematic behavior they've directly observed.

Understanding what they've observed will give you a good starting point to confirm there's an issue. There are a few ways to do this, depending on the type of product you're working with as well as the reported problem. First, I would check on the specific report to make sure that it does represent a bug. Just because the customer is reporting something wrong doesn't mean that's the case; maybe the product is just not acting in the way that he expects because of the way it's configured. If he says the service must be broken because he can't log in, perhaps his service is shut off because he canceled the credit card you have on file and all your emails telling him that his payment has failed went to spam. You're the expert on the product, so you should have a good idea of what might cause part of your product to behave in unexpected ways; go through those potential causes to try to nail down exactly what's happening.

Another approach is to attempt to replicate the problem yourself. This is often my preferred approach, because you can work in a controlled environment. If the customer says your product is doing something wrong, but it's working perfectly when you test it in a new, clean account that you've just created, that indicates that there's likely something in her account that's causing the issue. It may be that things aren't configured the way she expects, or it may be that you have a bug that only comes up in certain conditions, and those conditions are present in her environment. If you can't replicate the issue initially, try to change the settings on your account to match hers and replicate there. Having your own environment means you can keep making changes and testing things, which is really helpful in troubleshooting.

Evaluate the Problem

You've reviewed the customer account, and you're able to confirm that there's an issue - so far so good. Don't just jump straight into having engineering fix it, though. Your job as a PM is to prioritize things, including bugs, and to do that you need to understand it.

Your analysis of the issue should be across two dimensions - *who it's affecting* and the *impact on those users*. Who is obviously important; if you have a bug that's affecting one customer, it should be lower priority than a similar bug affecting all of your customers. Numbers aren't the only thing that matter, though, especially in enterprise software. When you're dealing with businesses, a bug that's affecting five customers may be much higher priority than a bug that's affecting fifty if those five customers are paying you $10 million a year each and the fifty are paying you $10,000. In consumer software, on the other hand, it's more likely that every user has roughly the same value to your company, so you'll probably only care about the number of people affected.

To determine who it's affecting, go through the data available to you. First, check with your support team and in their bug reporting software. If an issue has suddenly arisen that's affecting a lot of customers, your support team will be the first to know, so they can be a great resource. If they're filing tickets (or if customers are creating support tickets by emailing your support team about their issues), then searching your ticketing system will give you an idea of who is affected.

You can also tackle this question by starting with data. If you know what the symptom is, then try to go through the data available to you to see who else is having that symptom. This approach is similar to the previous question - if some of your customers are having trouble logging into your web app, then you can start by looking at how overall logins have changed since you started noticing the issue, then narrow it down to see which of your users aren't logging in.

As you assess who is impacted by the issue, make sure you keep records of them. If you're in the enterprise, make a list of individual customers. If you're serving consumers, keep track of which types of users are affected (e.g. is it users from a particular country, on a particular device, etc.). This will be very helpful later for making sure you're messaging the right people about the issue and the fix.

Once you know who is affected, you need to understand the impact. Just because a bug is affecting every single one of your customers doesn't mean it's a high priority. If the bug in question is a small, broken image in the footer of your web app, it's unlikely that anyone's going to be too upset about it. On the other hand, if a bug is only affecting one customer, but it's preventing that customer from logging in and using your app at all, that's a more significant problem.

As you evaluate the impact, there are a few things to consider:
1. What part of the product is impacted?
2. What is the effect of the issue on that part of the product?
3. Are there any workarounds?

Naturally, some parts of any product are more important than others. When I was making software for call centers, if our ability to make and receive calls stopped working, even for a small number of customers, we had to drop everything to fix it, because every minute it was down, our customers weren't able to get customer support calls. On the other hand, if our billing system went down, that could wait a week or two - nobody was going to complain if we billed them a little late. Knowing what is affected is the first step to understanding how significant the impact is.

The second thing to understand is the actual effect of the bug. If the billing system has a bug that means you aren't able to charge people, that's not great. On the other hand, if a the billing system has a bug that's charging customers $10,000 to their credit card on file at the top of every hour, that's a huge problem.

Make sure you understand what kind of effects comprise a serious issue. Outages of core functionality are obviously problematic, but another set of extremely important issues are those related to *data integrity*. Going back to the example of the call center software I worked on, if our reporting system went down, that was bad. A lot of customers planned the staffing of their call centers each month based on the data that we provided them, so if they weren't getting that data it meant they had to delay that planning.

You might think that the worst thing that can happen to a reporting system is an inability to report data, but that's often not the case. For us, it was much, much worse if the system was giving incorrect data than no data at all. If there's no data and a customer has to put off their planning until they're able to get the data, that's inconvenient, but if they plan out their call center staffing for the next month based on the wrong data, they might be grossly understaffed, in which case their customers will be angry, or grossly overstaffed, in which case they've spent more money than necessary. Both of those are significantly worse effects than inconvenience.

As you go through these types of bug-resolution questions with an interviewer, think critically about who their customers are and what type of issues are really going to negatively impact them.

The last thing I consider when evaluating a bug is whether or not there's a workaround. If your web app is having problems loading in Chrome, you can tell your customers to use another browser temporarily. It's annoying and inconvenient, but it's not the end of the world (unless your users are in a big enterprise that has highly restrictive IT policies that only let them use specific browsers - that's why it's important to know your users). If there is a way to still achieve the functionality they want, that's generally a mitigating factor, though depending on how difficult or time-consuming that workaround is, it may be more or less mitigating.

Prioritize a Fix for the Problem

Now that you know who is affected and how, you know almost everything that you need to in order to prioritize the fix. The last step is to create a ticket for the fix and have your engineering team estimate how much effort it will take.

Once you have the ticket ready, you have to figure out where it lies on the list of priorities. Since we understand the impact, we now have to go back to something I talked about much earlier in this book - company objectives. Remember that engineering effort you spend fixing bugs is engineering effort you aren't spending creating new features, so bugs aren't just prioritized against each other, they're also prioritized against new features you could be building. If you have a bug that's preventing people from logging into your product, that's going to be higher priority than any new feature (since those can't be used without logging in anyway). On the other hand, if you have an annoying bug that's affecting a lot of small customers, but you have a product launch deadline coming up that can't be moved, the bug will likely have to wait.

Since you won't have the hypothetical company roadmap in this problem, you won't really know how much of a priority a bug fix is, but that's fine. Just explain at a high level that your decision about how urgently to fix this bug will be informed by what else is being worked on, and how much fixing it will contribute to your overall company priorities.

One flaw of this system is that it often neglects very low-priority bugs. If we take an example I mentioned earlier, in which an image is broken in the footer of your web app, it's unlikely that fixing it will contribute to any major company objectives. Still, it's annoying and does look bad, so you want to get it done at some point. For that reason, I'm a big fan of bug weeks, where everyone in engineering just fixes bugs, and of having a rotation such that one person on each engineering team is always just handling bugs. Either is a helpful way to make sure that you don't end up with a backlog of low-priority bugs that never get addressed.

How would you set up a system for your support team to triage bugs that are reported to them?

This question is very much related to the last one, but it's generally targeted at people who are interviewing for more senior product management positions. Where an individual PM is going to be responsible for dealing with issues in her products, a more senior PM or a director/VP will be dealing with company-wide process.

For that reason, your system needs to consider the same things - who is affected, how significant is the impact, and are there any workarounds? The challenge here is that you need to quantify those things in a framework that's used by a lot of people with varying levels of technical sophistication.

The first step is to create a system, and the second is to train people to use it. The system needs to be as simple as possible without leaving out any important information. My preference is to have it rate each bug on three dimensions: *customers affected, impact* and *urgency*. As you can see, we're basically looking at the same set of information as when we're examining the bugs ourselves, but I've pulled out urgency as its own category. This is because in my experience, support really wants to be able to communicate along that specific dimension - if they can't highlight a bug that they think needs to be fixed ASAP, it ends up feeling like there's a gap in communication.

Affected customers is the easiest metric to quantify - for a consumer product, I would just take total percentage of your customer base affected, and for an enterprise product I would look at the contract value of all affected customers and take that as a percentage of your total contract value.

For impact and urgency, in order to keep things simple, I like a 1-4 scale for each. This enables me to give clear guidelines for what each value means. For example, for impact:

1. Very minor impact - No significant components of the product are affected
2. Minor impact - Significant components of the product are affected, but they are still usable
3. Major impact - Significant components of the product are unusable
4. Critical impact - Core functionality of the product is unusable

For urgency:

1. Very low urgency - Customers can go indefinitely with the issue in place without facing problems with the product.
2. Low urgency - Customers' experience is impacted in a somewhat negative way, but they are able to continue using the product.
3. High urgency - Customers are unable to use part of the product until the issue is fixed.
4. Critical urgency - Customers are unable to use core functionality until the issue is fixed.

Once I have those in place, I would have a simple equation to score the bug. First, we need to convert the affected customers into a number from one to four. To do this, I would create buckets. For a consumer product, this might look like:

- 1: 0-5% of customers affected

- 2: 5-10% of customers affected
- 3: 10-20% of customers affected
- 4: 20+% of customers affected.

For enterprise products, I would use a similar scale, but measure the total amount of revenue affected, not the number of customers.

From there, average the three numbers and round to the nearest whole number to get an overall score. A four is an absolute top-priority bug - engineering needs to drop everything and start working on it immediately, and a one is very low priority; it can wait until it's convenient to fix it (perhaps because someone is working on related code for a new feature).

That's just an example - as long as the framework captures the information you need to prioritize the bug as a product manager, then it's doing its job. That said, creating a framework is the easy part; getting people to use it correctly and consistently is much harder.

In order to ensure everyone is using the system, make it easy by providing them tools. My system above had a bunch of math in it (converting a percent to a 1-4 ranking, averaging numbers). You shouldn't make support reps do this; instead, create a bug form in which they enter the relevant numbers, and the math happens behind the scenes. This form can also collect other relevant information like their description of the bug - that way, if you integrate it with your bug tracking system, you can automatically create a ticket once the form is filled out.

You don't just have to make sure people are using it, though - you also have to make sure people are using it *consistently*. The 1-4 scale I proposed above for impact and urgency may be understood differently by different people. For that reason, I recommend having someone on the product team review the bugs before they go to engineering. First of all, that will prevent duplicates from being created, and second of all, it will allow a PM to adjust numbers that are off. Third, and most important, it gives one person a big-picture view of how everyone who uses the system is rating bugs, so he can see how consistently things are being used.

Until everyone is using it consistently, it's important to provide feedback. Rather than do this one bug at a time, work with customer support management to do this on a regular basis in front of the whole team. If there is a weekly support meeting, go to that and go through 3-4 bugs that came in over the last week, explaining how you would categorize them along each dimension and why. You'll still end up with some outliers when people file bugs, but providing examples will help to get everyone on the same page.

To sum up, you need to *create a prioritization framework, provide tools to make that framework easy to use*, and *create a feedback loop*.

PM INTERVIEW QUESTIONS - HOMEWORK

It can be very challenging to assess a PM's skills in an interview setting. Design questions and questions about past experience help, but ultimately they still leave the interviewer assessing the candidate on a host of skills without actually seeing her demonstrate those skills.

That's where homework can be incredibly helpful. That said, you'll hear many mixed feelings on the topic, both from interviewers and candidates. The big downside is of course that homework takes time from the candidate - potentially a lot of it. I have rejected interview requests because I wasn't interested enough in the company to spend time on the homework, and I have also had candidates decline to continue interviewing when they were given homework. This is arguably a good thing - after all, it ensures that you're only speaking with candidates are really interested - but it also means that you lose the chance to sell qualified applicants who might be great fits. One company I worked at finally chose to abandon homework as part of the interview process after we lost out on a couple of candidates we were very interested in because they didn't want to dedicate the time to it.

Personally, though, I think that homework is a good thing for the candidate, especially for those trying to find their first PM roles and those trying to transfer to a different type of company or PM role. Homework is one of the few opportunities you have to very concretely address a lack of experience by showing that you can tackle a real issue.

Homework Prompts

The type of homework given can vary, but generally it relates to the product or industry of the company where you're interviewing.

A few examples:

- I interviewed at a large ride-sharing company, and they asked me to think about a new line of business in which they would partner with employers to offer rides to and from work as a benefit. I was asked to pick some specific feature that would be needed for the product and to detail how I would go about implementing it.
- As an interviewer at a company that provided a marketplace to find attorneys, I asked candidates to determine whether it would also make sense for the company to expand into providing a similar marketplace for accountants. They were asked to describe how they determined whether that expansion would be a good idea, and if so what features we would need to roll out the accountant marketplace.
- As a candidate for a partner PM role at a video conferencing company, I was asked to consider which types of partners we should seek to integrate our product with. I was then asked to pick one of those partners and present on the features that an integration with that partner would need to be successful.

As you can see, each of these questions is a bit different, but they each relate to what the candidate will be working on and require him to address a specific product problem. The actual prompts varied greatly in length and detail - some described exactly what they wanted to see in the slides, while others didn't give much more detail than what's above.

The amount of detail you're given is a good indication of what you're being tested on. If you have very specific instructions, it's better to follow them than to try to go way above and beyond - the specificity means that your interviewers are looking for the particular set of things they're asking about.

A related example from my career - I was once asking a candidate about a vending machine for the blind (as described in an earlier chapter) and she ended up describing how she would build a food delivery service for underprivileged and disabled people. It was an intelligent and thorough answer but not about a vending machine, so I rejected her. I knew she was intelligent coming in, so it didn't matter that she'd proven her intellect. I was trying to understand how she would tackle a particular problem, and the answer that I got is that she would ignore the problem and do something that she thought was more valuable. A nice idea if she wanted to be a philanthropist, but not so much for a product manager. The same applies here - if the questions are specific, your answers should be on topic.

On the other hand, if you get a vague prompt (e.g. something ending in "describe how you would address this problem"), then the interviewer is looking to see whether you focus on the right things and include all the necessary information in a well-structured way. More on that below.

Presentation

I've written about the importance of structure before, but nowhere does it matter more than on homework. Because you have time in advance to plan your answer and create a presentation, it should have a clear, coherent structure that takes the interviewers through your thought process and solution. If you're constantly jumping back and forth during your presentation, you're not going to get the job.

You'll typically get some guidelines on your presentation - either a number of slides or an amount of time you have to present. Often, you'll hear that you should only spend a specified amount of time on the homework as well. While you should definitely keep the presentation to the number of slides and time allotted, spend as much time as you need at home - I've never seen an interviewer ding a candidate for having a thorough presentation that clearly took lots of time.

With that in mind, the overall structure of your presentation should virtually always be:

- Title slide
- Prompt
- Your answer to the prompt
- Assumptions you used
- Details about how you got to your answer
- Summary that restates your answer
- "Thank You" slide
- Appendix

While you will likely present your slides, this structure ensures that someone who receives it via email will be able to understand it without you speaking over it. This is important, as people may review it before your presentation (in which case they'll develop an opinion of it and you just based on what's on the slides - if it's a bad one, that's tough to overcome). It may also be forwarded after the fact if someone like the hiring manager's boss, who isn't included in the interview process, wants to learn about you.

Title and Prompt

The title is pretty self explanatory, but be sure it includes your name, since multiple candidates will be sending in presentations. The prompt should literally just be the exact prompt that you were given, quoted on the slide. This is because you may have people who aren't intimately familiar with the prompt - typically, I've had a couple of PMs, a designer and an engineer in the room for this kind of a presentation. This context was especially helpful for the engineers, since we would rotate a fair number of them into the process, so not all of them were very familiar with the prompt.

Assumptions

The assumptions slide is key. I'll caveat by saying that whether you need a specific slide depends on the prompt and your response - in some cases you might just want to include specific assumptions as they become relevant to your explanation - but you absolutely must have any assumptions you're using in there.

Assumptions are a key part of demonstrating your ability to break down the problem. Let's look at the above example of a partner PM at a videoconferencing company. It's asking which type of partners the company should work with, but without context, that's an impossible question to answer. Why are they bothering to partner with other companies? Is it to drive revenue? To increase awareness of their product through partner marketing? Is it because customers have been requesting integrations with other pieces of software they use?

Most prompts will leave a few important questions like that open. In some cases, they will direct you to make specific assumptions, while others will be unclear on that. If you're not sure, you should always email the person who gave you the assignment (and make sure you read the assignment when you get it, so you can email him immediately, not the night before you need to present) and ask whether they can provide the missing pieces of context, or whether you should make assumptions and fill them in yourself.

Some more junior candidates I've worked with have been nervous about emailing to ask, because they don't want to seem like they can't figure things out for themselves. Don't worry about this - as a PM, you're going to have to ask a lot of people a lot of questions to figure out what products to build. As a result, a lot of hiring managers expect you to ask questions about the prompt and will judge you negatively if you don't. There's nothing wrong with sending a quick email that says "Hi <hiring manager>, I just took a look at the prompt and had a quick question. It says that I should pick a partner to integrate with and present on features that would make an integration successful. Can you clarify how you would define success in that context (number of customers using the integration, revenue driven by the integration, marketing exposure as a result of the integration, etc.)? If not, I can lay out some assumptions about the definition of success at the beginning of my presentation and work based off of those. Thanks!"

If you get a response from the hiring manager with answers to your questions, be sure to include those in the assumptions section, and attribute them to the hiring manager. This is important, because you want other people in the room to understand that those assumptions didn't come from you, so it's not valuable to spend time discussing their merits.

If you're making your own assumptions, give at least some reason for why you made them (e.g. "I assumed that the goal of partnerships is to reduce churn [lost customers], because keeping customers is a critical driver of revenue, which is the ultimate goal of the business, and because in my experience in the past, partner integrations have done a much better job of lowering churn than bringing in new customers.").

Try not to spend too much time discussing your assumptions. If people ask questions about why you made certain assumptions, it's fine to answer them, but it's also completely fine to explain that these assumptions are just intended to fill in gaps in the prompt, so you can give a more thorough answer. Let them know you recognize they might not be right, and certainly if you were encountering a similar problem in the real world, you'd do the research to make sure that you had the correct assumptions before proceeding.

Details

I'm using the general term "details" here, because this is the part of your presentation that's going to vary most depending on the prompt and any restrictions on length and time. Basically, this is where you're going to lay out how you got to your answer. I've talked about structuring your answers well, and this is one of the most important places to do that. You should tell a story that follows a logical path from the prompt to your solution. In order you do this, you should break down the prompt into a logical set of pieces that you can address one at a time.

I'm going to use the above prompt about a videoconferencing company as an example. Here it is, with the relevant pieces that you would need to address, bolded:

- As a candidate for a partner PM role at a video conferencing company, I was asked to consider **which types of partners we should seek to integrate our product with**. I was then asked to **pick one of those partners** and present on the **features that an integration** with that partner would **need to be successful**.

Let's start from the beginning - you need to figure out which partners you'd integrate with. Remember, though, that the point is to walk the panel through your thought process, so don't just start with a list of companies that you think would make good partners. Instead, talk through how you got to those companies. I would start with major software categories. For example, a videoconferencing service could benefit from integrations with a few types of companies:

- Calendaring and scheduling (since most videoconferences are for scheduled meetings that go on the calendar)
- Conference room management software (since most VC units are in conference rooms)
- HR/IT management software (since a company paying for VC software will want to ensure new employees get access to it immediately, while employees that leave automatically see their access revoked)
- Internal analytics tools (so the company can understand

how much people are using the VC software to understand if it's a good investment)
- Communications tools (to allow people to quickly start a video conference if they're already chatting via text on a tool like Slack or Microsoft Teams and want to move to video)

Starting with this level of breadth allows the panel to see that you're taking a holistic approach and then narrowing down, rather than just picking the first idea you have and running with it.

Next, pick one of those categories, but start with explaining the criteria you're using to make your selection. That criteria should either be from the prompt or should have been laid out as an assumption. For example, if you've stated that your assumption was that the goal of partnering is to reduce churn, then quickly run through each of the categories and explain how they might or might not do that.

In this case, I would point out that all of the above categories could contribute to churn reduction - making it easy to schedule meetings, integrating videoconferencing software with conference rooms, and enabling people to launch video calls from their other communication tools will the product easier for employees to use, which will likely drive more usage. Enabling easy provisioning and deprovisioning through HR/IT management integrations will both make it easier for employees to get started and reduce cost and risk by making sure that ex-employees can't keep using the software.

I believe, though, that the best choice here is an integration with internal analytics tools. Ultimately, it's great if the product is easy to use, but what really matters is whether management believes that this videoconferencing product is adding more value than it costs to pay for. The only way for them to really know that is to have analytics - if people are using the product a lot, but management doesn't see that, they might still not want to renew it. On the other hand, if they can see a chart showing them that employees are taking hundreds of meetings a day over video, they'll know that there is value there. Even in the bad case, where analytics show that people aren't using it heavily, you'll likely hear complaints from the client early in their contract period, so you have time to work with their employees to find out why they aren't using it. If there are solvable problems, then the customer's analytics tool will be able to show usage growing over time as you solve them, so you don't lose the customer from their bad initial impression.

I'll stop here to say that I have an above average handle on this prompt, because I worked at an enterprise videoconferencing company in a partner PM role, so this is the kind of stuff I thought about every day. You probably won't have my same level of background, which is fine (good interviewers won't expect you to). If you're having trouble getting started on a prompt like this, though, check out competitors of the company where you're interviewing. For this prompt, I would look up videoconferencing companies and see what they've integrated with. Luckily, you can find a great example of all of Blue Jeans' (the VC company I worked at, though I can't take credit for their app network) partners at https://www.bluejeans.com/app-network, broken down by category. This won't work for every prompt, but it never hurts to try to find real-life examples of the prompt you've been given.

Now that I've narrowed it down to one category, I need to pick a specific partner. Again, rather than just give my answer, I would start a level up and talk about a few of the potential partners in the analytics space. Again, if you're not familiar with the space, Google is your friend (though if possible, try to pick something you are familiar with). In this case, there are plenty of examples - I'd probably list Tableau, Looker, MicroStrategy and Domo, but don't worry if you aren't familiar with them.

Once again, when making a selection of one of them, I want to walk through why I made that selection, always bringing things back to the initial objective of churn reduction. In this case, I'd say that the best way to reduce churn through this kind of integration is to pick the one that can be used by most of our customers. In real life, I would survey all of our customers about what analytics tools they use to get that answer. Since that's not possible for the prompt, I would explain that I'm selecting the one with the most overall market share, which in this case is Tableau (you can find this pretty easily online).

This is likely when you're going to start getting questions that make you defend your choices. If you present a list of five companies you might integrate with, make sure you've given some thought to all of them - don't just pick your answer and slap four other companies on there to fill the slide. I'll often ask something like, "What other approach besides market share might you take to making this decision?" That's open ended enough that if the interviewee really thought about the problem, they should be able to come up with something. If they started from the answer and then just filled in everything else, they'll struggle.

By the way, another approach you might take is to find the top three most used analytics tools among your customers, then have your engineers review each of their technical documentation and estimate how much effort would be for each of them. That would enable you to start with the integration that you can build the fastest, so you can get a real product into the hands of your customers and see if it has the effects on churn that you expect. You might also do a deep analysis of previous churn, and try to figure out what types of customers tend to complain about not having enough insight into whether people are using your product. Then, instead of looking at your entire customer base, just look at those folks who have the exact problem you're trying to solve, see what analytics tool most of them use, and go with that. There are plenty of ways to analyze a problem like this, and your panel will want to see that you can think through it a few different ways.

If you end up deep in a discussion here about different approaches, that's a good thing. Interviewers want to know that you can take feedback and be flexible in how you think about a problem. In a real PM job, you're going to have a lot of conversations with people of different backgrounds and different levels about how to approach a given problem, so if you're having that kind of discussion with your panel, that's a good thing. That said, always keep an eye on time. You're the presenter, so you're responsible for driving the conversation. If the conversation has gone off on a tangent, it's up to you to remind everyone that you only have a certain amount of time left, so you'd like to move on (but of course you're happy to answer further questions at the end). Again, in real life, it's largely going to be your job to control these kinds of conversations and make sure that everyone stays focused on what they need and gets to answers in a reasonable amount of time. Showing that you have control of the room in the interview demonstrates a very relevant skill.

Once you've picked a partner, you'll now need to get into the details of how you would integrate. For an integration of a video tool with an analytics tool, this means understanding what data is going to be sent to the analytics tool. As always, start from the overall goal - if your objective is to reduce customer churn, what data should customers see to achieve that? I won't go too far into the weeds here, but the answer is likely something like how many meetings are happening in a given time, how many people are in those meetings and how long the meetings last. This prompt specifies that you should define how those features will make an integration successful, but many will just tell you to describe features you'd implement. Whether they state it or not, the goal of anything in your product should be to serve your overarching objective, so it's critical to explain how every feature you present does so.

For any prompt that asks about specific features of a product, one thing I strongly recommend is showing a basic prioritization framework. Take all the features you think should go into the product, and rank them from P0 (absolutely critical - the product won't work without it) to P2 (nice to have but not essential). In practice, rankings will often go to P3 or P4, but for this kind of a presentation it usually doesn't make sense to talk about anything below P2.

Example:

Priority	Feature
P0	Tableau can display how many meetings were held in a given timeframe
P0	Tableau can display average meeting length
P0	Tableau can display average number of participants per meeting
P1	Tableau can break down number of meetings, average length and average participant numbers by which department hosted the meeting

The real list would be longer than this, but this should give you an idea. As I walk through this, I would explain that basic, high-level statistics around meeting usage are critical to the product. Those are the most fundamental things a customer would need to know to see if the product is being used, so they're the features we absolutely must have at launch. Being able to break things down by department is great as well - it would be really useful to understand that marketing is using the product a ton but sales isn't touching it - but we can launch the product and add that first thing after launch.

If you include this kind of a list, it's definitely going to trigger criticism and discussion about your prioritization choices.

Again, this is okay! If panelists disagree with your choices, it's okay to defend them or to push back - just think about what they're saying and give an honest answer that you believe in.

Summary

Your summary slide should restate your answer, and you should use it as an opportunity to go back through your presentation in a few sentences. This is important, because there were probably distractions and questions, so taking 30 seconds to walk people through what you've said one more time will hammer home your message and leave them with the impression that you're thoughtful and organized.

For this prompt, I would summarize by saying something like, "The prompt asked me to determine a partner we should integrate with and to describe features of that integration that would make it successful. I began by assuming that success would be defined by reduced churn among existing customers. I then examined a number of possible categories of partners and landed on analytics tools, because I feel that an integration between analytics and videoconferencing can provide insights to customers that make them understand the value of our service, which will reduce their likelihood of churn. After looking at the top competitors in the analytics space, I selected Tableau because it has the greatest market share, though if I were approaching this problem in real life, I would find out who has the greatest market share among our customers, not just overall in the market. I decided that the critical features for launch are high-level usage metrics, since those are the most important things a customer would need to determine if the product is being used. Since customers seeing good usage are unlikely to churn, this is key to our overall goal. Finally, I would build out more granular information over time, starting with the ability to sort the high-level metrics by department."

Thank You

After your summary, include a slide that says "Thank you!"

That's it. It just clearly communicates that you're done with your presentation to avoid any awkwardness that might arise if people think you have more slides coming up. It's a minor thing, but it helps keep things smooth and positive. When you get to this slide, you should thank everyone for their time and ask if they have any more questions.

Appendix

When approaching a PM homework problem, often times you'll think through it, come up with a great solution, and then realize you've got too much detail and your presentation is too long. If that happens, don't get rid of the extra content, just move it to the appendix. You don't need to present any of this, but if questions come up, it looks really impressive when you can go to a slide in the appendix that shows that you thought through them deeply and came up with answers.

For a presentation like the one above, the appendix might include more details on your research on industries and companies within that industry (e.g. since you told them Tableau has the most market share, you might have an appendix slide breaking down all the competitors by their market share and citing where you go those numbers). It might also include more detail about prioritization. For example, you may wish to focus on five or six key features - in that case, it often makes sense to add an appendix with a more detailed list of all the features you've talked about. That way, when a panelists suggests a feature that you considered but didn't include, you can skip to the relevant appendix slide and let them know you agree completely but omitted it for time, but that you're happy to go over the full list of features you considered after the presentation if there's time.

Other Tips for Your Presentation

A good structure and a well-thought-through answer to the prompt are the biggest pieces of making your presentation a success, but they're not the only ones. Because the job of any product manager involves making and presenting a whole lot of slide decks, you'll be judged on the quality of your slides as well. If you haven't made a lot of decks in your life, there are lots of good books out there about how to make them well, so I won't go into a lot of detail here. That said, here are a few tips on creating an engaging deck for this kind of presentation.

The first piece of advice I'll offer is probably the most common one about making slide decks - don't just fill slides up with a ton of text. You can find lots of rules about how much text is allowable on the internet, but there's no perfect answer. Just make sure that when you pull up a slide, it's not a huge mass of text that's tough to focus on. That's not to say you should have nothing but pictures - remember, this deck will probably be sent around to people who won't have the benefit of hearing your presentation, so it should be at least basically comprehensible on its own. Make sure, though, that your text is only hitting the main points (you can add extra context while speaking) and that it's broken up visually.

There are lots of ways to make text look better on a slide. First, if you need to have a significant amount of text, use text formatting to draw your viewers' eyes to the most important pieces and to break it up visually. For example, if you wanted to talk about why you chose Tableau, it's pretty apparent which of these two options would look better on a deck:

Option 1

Tableau is the clear leader in its market. It was founded in 2003, and it's now a publicly traded company with a market cap of almost $10B. It has over 86,000 customers across a wide range of industries. Its customer base is twice as large as its next biggest competitor.

Option 2

Tableau

- Leader in its market
- Founded 2003

- Publicly traded company with a **market cap of almost $10B**
- Currently has about **86,000 customers**
- Customer base is twice as large as its next biggest competitor

Our second option is easier to read because of the bullet points, and it draws attention to the most relevant pieces of information. The main goal here is to point out that Tableau is the right choice for us due to its market share, so we're highlight its size and customer base.

There's more you can do with visuals, though. You should find logical places to include images to make your slides easier on the eye. Let's try a third option for this slide:

- Leader in its market
- Founded 2003
- Publicly traded company with a **market cap of almost $10B**
- Currently has about **86,000 customers**
- Customer base is twice as large as its next biggest competitor

Notable Customers

As you can see, one of the easiest ways to add some visual interest to slides is by replacing company names with logos. In this case, I've just taken the above information, formatted it nicely, and swapped out Tableau's name for its logo. Additionally, the "Notable Customers" section at the bottom is a way to highlight my overall point (we should integrate with Tableau because of their customer base), while making the slide more visually appealing. This looks clean and polished, and it's informative even without the context of you speaking over it, all without too much text.

Company logos are really visuals for the sake of visuals - they don't convey more information than just writing the company name down, but they're more aesthetically pleasing than plain text. For the right prompt, though, you should also include functional visuals - images that convey important information better than text would. The most common example for a PM homework presentation is mockups. Most products and features have visual components, and it's almost always better to show than tell, especially because you'll have to do the same in a typical PM job. When creating a product spec, I'll often make a quick sketch on the whiteboard to help show people what I have in mind.

Not all homework prompts will lend themselves to mockups, but where possible, try to find a way to include them. If your homework asks you to design a feature, and you have a few potential options in mind, lean towards the ones that allow for better visuals in your presentation.

If you're not an artist, don't worry - your visuals don't have to be pretty, they just have to convey information. It's absolutely fine to just sketch something on a piece of paper or a simple drawing program, since that's what you'd likely do in the real job anyway!

Here's a simple visual of the features from our presentation:

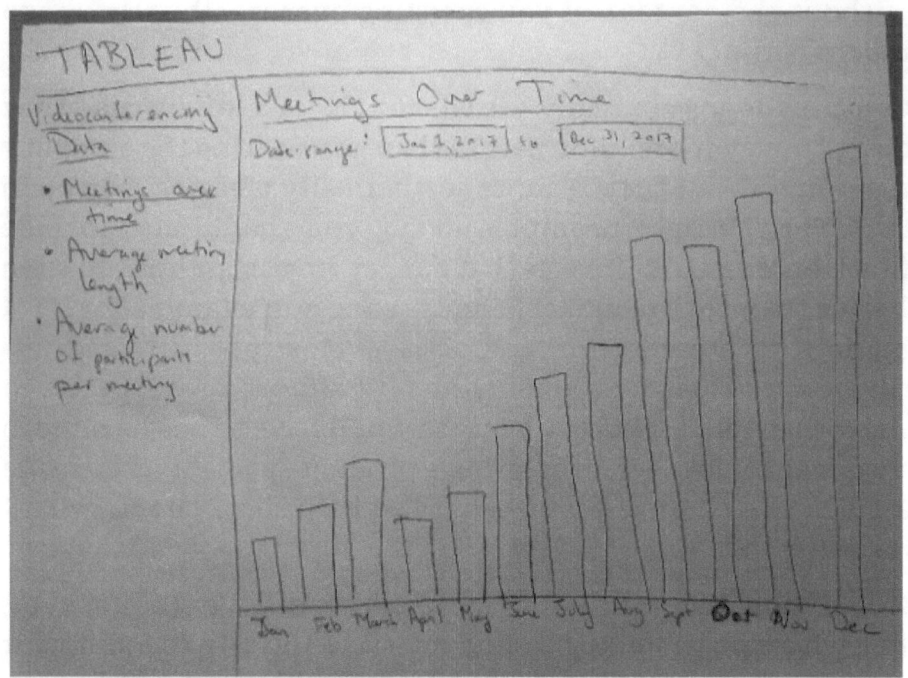

As you can see, this isn't especially beautiful - that's okay! You're not interviewing to be a designer, so the purpose of mockups isn't to show a beautiful design, it's to convey information visually for ease of understanding. In the real world, your designer is going to take a drawing like this and then create the actual designs your engineers will use to implement it.

You can see how this adds a lot of information to the feature it's showing (the ability of Tableau to display the number of meetings happening over a particular time frame). It shows that we need a way to select the time frame, it shows that we're going to use a bar graph for this, and it shows the general layout of the screen. This leaves much less to the imagination than a text description of the feature, and the less you leave to the imagination, the more likely your product is to turn out as you had imagined it.

One final but incredibly important note on visuals in slide decks: USE A TEMPLATE. It baffles me when people show up with a presentation that is just black Times New Roman text on a white background. Microsoft PowerPoint and Google Slides both come with free templates that will make your presentation look more professional with one click.

I'm sure you'll agree with me that one of these looks much better than the other:

> **BigCompany Homework Assignment**
> Alex Willen

> **BigCompany Homework Assignment**
> Alex Willen

All the second one took was one click.

Practical Preparation

Finally, there are a few practical considerations to make your presentation go as smoothly as possible. First, make sure that you have everything you need to present - don't rely on the company where you're presenting to have anything more than a TV and an HDMI cable. That means that if you don't have an HDMI port on your laptop, you need to bring a converter. In case you don't know what I'm talking about, I mean one of those little white dongles you use to connect to a TV. It's not the end of the world if you don't - companies should have this kind of thing on hand - but if you run into a case where they're disorganized and someone has taken the dongle out of the room, you look prepared and save time if you already have one in your bag.

Beyond that, you should obviously have your laptop and charger with you. You should also have multiple, redundant copies of your presentation. If they ask you to send your presentation ahead, don't assume they'll be able to find it when you get there. You should have a copy of it stored to your hard drive in case you get there in case their internet is down. I also recommend printing a few paper copies of your presentation - this can be a lifesaver if you get there only to find that their TV is broken, the conference room has been double booked or you end up in a weirdly shaped room where no one can see the TV. All of these issues would be the fault of the company, but they also provide an opportunity to exhibit your preparedness.

QUESTIONS FROM YOU

I've mentioned a few times that interviewing is a two way street, and I mean that seriously. You're evaluating the possibility of spending eight (or more) hours a day working for each company you're interviewing at, so you shouldn't settle for the first job you interview for.

Companies know this, and that's why they leave you time to ask questions. In fact, you should take note of how they approach this, because the level of emphasis they put on making sure you get the information you need tells you something about their culture. Great interviewers create a conversational atmosphere, so you feel as comfortable asking questions as they do.

On the other hand, I have had interviews in which the interviewer had a very regimented set of questions that took up 55 minutes, and he left me a hurried five at the end for questions. That's a red flag in my book - not necessarily a dealbreaker, but certainly not a sign that you're talking to someone who treats informing you as a priority.

Your time for questions isn't just for you, though - as with anything you do during an interview, you're being evaluated. If an interviewer asks if you have any questions and you don't, that's a signal to the company that you aren't particularly interested or engaged in the process. After all, if you really cared about what the company was doing, you'd be excited about the opportunity to learn more about it, right?

For that reason, you shouldn't just consider what information you'll receive from the answer to a question you ask, but also what information it conveys to the interviewer. Well-informed questions are a great way to demonstrate that you've done your research on the company and that you have domain expertise.

They also demonstrate experience. When I ask an engineering manager how they structure their engineer teams, I offer up some context alongside - namely, that I've worked at companies that have structured their engineering teams differently and have put significant thought into what structure works best at different stages of a company's life.

I'm going to discuss questions that you should ask at different stages of the interview process. I'll assume the structure of the process is a first phone screen with a recruiter followed by a phone screen with a hiring manager and then an on site. Remember that you don't need to use the questions here; I certainly think they're good ones, but you should also consider what it is that's important to you when you consider a company and make sure you get that information too.

RECRUITER PHONE SCREEN

The initial phone screen with a recruiter will just cover the basics, so it's not the time to ask deep questions about the company's strategy and finances. That said, it's a good time to collect straightforward information about the company's size and structure. If I'm interviewing at a few places, I like to keep an Excel spreadsheet of basic company info and use this time to fill in any gaps.

How many people work at your company?

As someone who tends to interview at early-stage companies, this is important. There's a big difference between a 100 person company and a 300 person company. If you're interviewing at a tech behemoth, the answer is going to be in the thousands or tens of thousands, so you may just want to skip this.

How many people are on your product, engineering and design teams?

This one is important, because it tells you about the ratio of product to engineering and design. If there is one PM to every hundred engineers, that's a red flag. A good ratio is usually six to eight engineers to one product manager, though there are good reasons for it to be higher, so if the numbers sound off, ask if there's some particular reason for it.

Maybe they just brought on a new VP of product and were waiting for her to start before aggressively hiring PMs, so the ratio will come down soon. Also, if it's a highly technical product, there may be engineers working on infrastructure or other areas that don't really require significant product oversight.

If the number of engineers per PM sounds too high, ask how many engineers you'd be directly working with. You may hear a reasonable response, or you may hear that each PM is expected to manage three teams of ten (in which case I would advise you to run the other way).

Usually a good ratio of PM to design is one to one, but again, that can vary (and frankly great designers are tough to find, so it's rare to see that ratio in practice).

If either the number of engineers or designers concerns you, keep a note of that - if you continue along the process, you should have a chance to ask engineers, designers and product managers about how the relative sizes of their groups affects everyone's ability to get work done.

How would you describe your company culture?

Culture is one of the toughest things to assess in an interview, and it's certainly easier in person than over the phone. Still, I think this is a question worth asking because if culture is a point of focus for the executive team, their recruiters will know that and will want to talk about it.

More and more companies are increasingly putting a focus on culture by creating an explicit set of values that they follow. If this is the case, the recruiter will tell you what these are, and that should be telling. "Move fast and break things" is very different than "always think about the customer first." One isn't inherently different from the other, but knowing the company's values lets you figure out if they align with your own.

Why did you join <company>?

I like this question because it will tell you about culture in a different way. For me, the most important thing at any company is the people, so if the recruiter says that he knew the CEO (or someone else important) from a previous job and thought he was extraordinary, that's a positive sign. On the other hand, maybe you'd be more excited to hear that the recruiter joined the company because he was passionate about its mission. Whatever you're looking for in a company, this will give you a little bit more of a personal lens on its people.

What are you looking for in this role?

This is a really important question to ask, because it will give you useful information for subsequent interviews. Knowing what they want out of a candidate will allow you to focus your answers and highlight the right things on your resume. Whether they are looking for someone with a strong analytical background or someone who has experience at a company that's grown quickly, this information will help you make sure that you have all the right anecdotes ready for when you talk to the hiring manager and the rest of the team.

HIRING MANAGER PHONE SCREEN

Once the recruiter has covered the basics, if he feels that you might be a good fit, he'll pass you along to the hiring manager. She will usually be the person you'd report to if you were hired for the role, and her goal here will be to assess if you're likely enough to be a good fit that it's worth bringing you on site to talk to more people.

Since she has more product management expertise than the recruiter, this screen will go into more detail about your previous experience and thoughts on product management. Hopefully you asked the recruiter what they're looking for in a candidate, because that's exactly what the hiring manager is going to be looking for now.

This is an ideal time to get into some detail about the product management team and their process, as well as to find out what kind of a manager you'd be reporting to. Phone screens are often just a half hour, so you won't necessarily have time to go especially deep. Still, two or three good questions can tell you a lot about what kind of an environment you'd be walking into if you took the job.

How do you structure the areas of responsibility that your PM team owns, and how much overlap is there between those areas of responsibility?

Some companies have products that are easily segmented into distinct and separate areas of responsibility. Each PM can work on his own product's roadmap, and product leadership gives big-picture guidance to the whole team.

On the other hand, at many companies this isn't possible - if the whole product is just one web app, for example, there's a lot more likely to be overlap between areas of responsibility and dependencies among product managers. That's not necessarily a problem, per se, but in that kind of an environment you really need to make sure that the company has the right kind of culture and communication in place. If you have a bunch of product managers who are only focused on their own areas, but you're relying on them to prioritize work that you need done to meet your objectives, you're not going to be in a great situation.

If it is something where PMs have significant dependencies on each other, ask how those are managed? What system is in place to determine whose priorities are more important when conflict arises? If you have strong leadership with clear objectives, that helps mitigate any potential issues, but if PMs are just left to sort things out among themselves, there's a lot of ways that can turn out badly.

The other thing I'd advise is that if areas of responsibility overlap a lot, make sure you're comfortable with the other product managers. Hopefully you'll get time to talk to them during an on site, but if that doesn't happen, you can always ask the hiring manager to set up coffee/lunch with some folks on the team after an offer is made. No one will turn that request down, since it gives them another opportunity to sell you on the job.

How would you describe your management style?

A good manager can make the difference between loving your job and hating it. That said, not everyone has the same definition of good. If you're more independent and experienced, you may want someone who's going to give you big-picture guidance and leave you to do your job. If you're younger or focused on developing some particular aspect of your career, you may prefer someone who's more hands-on.

Whatever your preference, make sure that the person who's going to be managing you is a good match for it. If you're dealing with someone who has only been promoted into management relatively recently, you can also ask questions about experience - how long has she been a manager, and how many people has she managed? If you're not fully comfortable with the answers, make a note to yourself to follow up on site. You can discuss further with the manager, and you can also ask her direct reports how they would describe her style to see if it matches with her own description.

What do your interactions with other departments look like? What processes do you have in place to work with them?

The product team sits at the center of everything and should be communicating with just about every other department. PMs have information critical to marketing, sales, customer success, support and certainly engineering and design.

That said, it's easy to go overboard with meetings as a result. If the whole product team has weekly meetings with each other department, that can take up a lot of hours every week. Add that to the time you need to be spending in meetings with your engineering counterparts, and suddenly half your week is in scheduled meetings.

Make sure that there's a good stream of communication among departments, but also that communication isn't just facilitated by overly burdensome process. How much process is too much will vary from company to company (generally, the smaller the company, the less process is necessary), so set your own expectations accordingly.

What's the product development process?

These days, the answer to this question will likely just be letting you know how closely the company follows the agile methodology. Not always, though.

The product development process will tell you something about the culture of the company - if you're working on two week sprints and deploying as soon as a feature is ready to go, it tells you the company emphasizes speed and agility. If they have a significant security and infrastructure review process before anything is deployed, that indicates that the company is more conservative.

Again, there's not a right or wrong answer here. If you're an early-stage consumer startup, speed is likely good. A network security company, on the other hand, probably shouldn't be letting engineers deploy new code any time. Make sure that the answer not only aligns with what you've been told about company culture, but also that it makes sense for the type of product you're dealing with.

ON SITE INTERVIEW

This is where things get more interesting - you'll be talking to a range of folks that might include anyone from junior engineers to the CEO. That means you have an opportunity to get a wide range of perspectives on the culture, process and anything else you want to know about the company. If you come prepared with a useful set of questions, you can leave with a lot of valuable information that will make it easy to evaluate if this is a company you want to work for.

Since you'll be engaging with folks from several departments, I'm going to break these questions down by role.

Product Management

There should be at least one, and ideally two or three, product managers on the interview schedule besides the hiring manager. These are your peers and the people you're going to be working with every day, so they need to have the chance to evaluate you and vice versa.

A lot of the phone screen questions for the hiring manager are also good for PMs at the on site. I try to ask everyone how they would describe the culture, because if I get three different answers from three different PMs, that's a red flag. I also like to talk through process more than once. Especially at early stage companies, each PM may have a different way of engaging with his engineering team. That shows trust from management and flexibility, but it can add logistical challenges. If you're going to be expected to define the process for working with your team, make sure that's something you're comfortable with.

Have you killed any products at this company? If so, why? If not, how would you decide to kill a product?

Many startups want to experiment with lots of new things, and rightly so - their size gives them an agility and ability to get new products out to market quickly that can make this a great strategy. To be successful, though, a company has to be disciplined about killing off products that don't work. Anything that stays alive takes resources to maintain, and those resources aren't going to the core product or to new things. That means that leaving every experiment alive indefinitely creates a huge tax on product and engineering that can kill a company.

The answer here will tell you a lot about discipline. What I want to hear when I ask this is that whenever they launch a new product, especially those they consider experimental, they have a set of KPIs they plan to measure and a specific time period for evaluation. At the end of that period, the stakeholders get together, review the KPIs and information about the product, and then make a decision about whether to keep investing in it or kill it off. This structure forces the PM and other stakeholders to critically evaluate products instead of just letting them limp along.

How do you engage with customers and how often?

A good product manager should be passionate about talking to both users and prospective users in a meaningful way. Dictating roadmaps without feedback from the people they're ultimately designed to serve is a recipe for disaster. If the PMs you talk to treat interaction with users as a burden, take that as a red flag.

I like to ask how they engage because it gives you a sense of commitment. Different types of organizations will have different ways of getting user feedback, but any type of user engagement can have varying levels of depth.

At consumer companies, user testing is the norm. This can

mean anything from showing friends and family a new product before it goes out and getting their feedback to doing A/B testing on millions of users. For companies operating at a very large scale, there should be a solid A/B testing framework that's in place that makes it easy for PMs to test minor changes. For new products, having a testing lab in which users come in for paid interviews is a good sign of a commitment to strong user engagement.

Enterprise software is a bit different, since it's important not just that end users have a good experience, but also that the executives that are making the decision about whether to buy your software feel that it fits their needs. Make sure PMs are addressing both of these things - too often, enterprise PMs spend all of their time in meetings with executives but neglect the actual users of their product. It's important to have those meetings, but also to go on site to customers and see how people are using software. When I was a PM for call center software, I spent at least a few hours a month just sitting in call centers, watching agents use the product. There's no substitute for that.

Tell me about something interesting you're working on.

The real goal of this question is to get a feel for how much passion the product manager you're talking to feels for her work. It certainly doesn't hurt to get an example of what passes for interesting at her company, but the real goal is to judge whether the PMs are excited by what they're working on.

If she struggles to come up with an answer, that's a huge red flag. If she just goes into a monotone description of what she's working on, that's also a red flag.

On the other hand, if she launches into an impassioned speech about not just what it is she's building, but the problem that she's solving and the way that she's making things better for her users, that's a great sign. Product management is a job that can be frustrating and draining at the best of times, so you want to be surrounded by people with the passion to work through some of the day-to-day drudgery and still be excited.

What are the biggest problems you're running into as a product organization lately?

The goal here is twofold - first, you should genuinely want to know what problems are coming up, because you're going to have to deal with them if you come on board. Different issues can make for very different work environments: a software company selling to a highly regulated industry that's having problems getting their product approved by regulatory agencies is very different than one where the user base is growing too fast for the infrastructure to keep up.

Beyond that, though, this is a chance to show what kind of value you can add. If you don't have any good thoughts on their problems, you can always just nod your head and say "interesting." If, on the other hand, they're facing problems that you have experience with, you've created a great opportunity to offer up solutions.

If you hear that the product team is having trouble getting data on their KPIs, and you've helped to create a data warehouse and set up an analytics tool on top of that, you're suddenly a much more attractive candidate. Product management is a discipline that constantly faces uncertain and ambiguous problems, and people who are able to solve those bring a lot of value to the table (which won't hurt when you're negotiating salary, either).

What's the worst thing about working at <company>?

This is actually a good question to ask all your interviewers, so you can compare their answers. That said, it's most important for PMs, since their pains are the most likely to be your pains if you start working there.

The first thing to look for is how quickly someone answers. If you get an immediate response, that tells you that they've been spending time thinking about the bad parts of their job, and people tend to do that when they're unhappy. Of course, if they pause and say it's a tough question, that might just be an act, but it's better than the alternative. I've had a couple of experiences during which interviewers took this question as an opportunity to vent about all the things that are bothering them at work - that's about the biggest red flag there is in my book.

The second thing to look for is, obviously, the answers. Don't let the answer get away with funny, cop-out type answers (e.g. we don't have catered food/we only have three flavors of La Croix/there's no ping pong table). If they try, politely press for more - just smile, say "I can't believe that's the worst thing in the company!" and then sit silently. For this question (and generally with any hard questions you ask), silence is key - let them think about the answer for as long as they need and don't break the silence first, even if it's a little awkward.

Legitimate answers can run the gamut - maybe there's poor communication, confusion about management structures, low wages, long hours, a lack of recognition for good work or just about anything else. What matters is whether the things those people see as problems are also problems for you. If people complain about a lack of resources, but you come from a startup environment and are used to being scrappy, maybe that's not a huge deal. On the other hand, if the hours are long, and work/life balance is very important to you, perhaps you should consider a different company.

Finally, if you're asking multiple people, consider the consistency of their answers. If they're all over the place, that's not a great sign, as it means that there are a number of problems. On the other hand, if you're hearing the same answer multiple times, ask one of the later interviewers what they think should be done about the problem and whether they feel progress is being made on it. If multiple people agree that there's something wrong at the company, but they don't feel that anything is being done, that means they're either afraid to bring it up to management, they don't know who to bring it up to or they've brought it up and feel that they've been ignored. All of those are bad things.

On the other hand, if they can point out concrete things that management has done to improve the problem, and they can describe what's going to be done moving forward, that's great! All companies have problems, but if management is listening to employees and taking action to fix them, then you've probably got a good culture of communication and respect for employees.

Engineering

You should be meeting with engineering while you're interviewing - one person at the very least, but ideally an engineering manager and an engineer. If you leave an on site without ever speaking to anyone from that department, take it as a red flag and let the recruiter know that if they're interested in moving forward after the on site that you'll want to grab coffee with an engineer who you'd be working with.

Engineers and product managers are tied at the hip. As a PM, if the engineers are bad, your products are going to be bad. If they're hard to work with, your day-to-day life is going to be unpleasant. You can make some assessment of the quality of their work by testing the products they've built, but you need to meet them to know if you're going to work well together.

The biggest theme of these questions is that they're designed to find the pain points of engineering, because more often than not, those are going to be your problems to solve.

If I were hired and started next week, what's something I could do that would make your life easier?

Just as engineers can make PMs' lives tough, the opposite is also true. A product manager who will give vague specs and cast blame on the engineering team when things go wrong is a nightmare. For that reason, it's good to convey that you see yourself as a resource to support engineering, and this question does that.

It also helps you understand the relationship between engineering and product management. Maybe there just aren't enough PMs and the engineers you'd be working with want guidance that isn't coming. Maybe expectations aren't being set well, and the executives are unhappy with the engineering team's performance even though it's good. Whatever the answer is, you'll learn something useful about the organization.

The last benefit of this question is that much like the last PM question above, it gives you an opportunity to show the kind of value you can add by talking about how you might address their issues. If the answer you get back is that bugs are handled haphazardly and often interrupt engineering work, you can talk about how you solved the same issue at a previous company by implementing a bug triage process in which any bug that would interrupt a sprint has to go through product management before engineering sees it. People who see you as someone with concrete solutions to their real problems will be excited to work with you.

How does product prioritize technical tasks like infrastructure work compared to features? Do you think they have struck a good balance between the two?

Balancing product and infrastructure work is one of the big challenges that faces product managers regularly. In many ways, you're comparing apples and oranges - how do you decide whether moving to a new framework is higher or lower priority than rolling out a new feature?

While it may be enlightening to hear their specific solution to this problem, what I'm really trying to gauge here is whether engineering feels there's a good balance being struck. Some product orgs tend to discount the importance of technical tasks, pushing new features out constantly until something in the system breaks, then dropping everything to fix it. That's not a good way to run a software company - it's inefficient, and it gets extremely frustrating for engineers who warn of the possible consequences ahead of time and get ignored, only to have to deal with those very consequences once they arise.

I'm a big believer in trying to quantify and understand the impact of technical tasks to make them easier to compare to features. If some technical task is going to enable me to add another 50 million users to my product, then I can assess the business impact of it and make a good decision.

When engineering tells me they have something important to work on, I try to find out what the benefit of doing it is, what the downside of not doing it is, and whether there are any alternatives. Even with that information, these kinds of decisions are more an art than a science, but asking those questions at least ensures that engineering has an opportunity to be heard.

How involved is engineering in planning the product roadmap?

Again, a big part of what I'm looking for here is whether the engineer I'm speaking to feels that she has an appropriate amount of input. While planning a roadmap should be primarily a responsibility of the product team, engineering can provide a lot of value, both by pointing out technical challenges of potential features and by getting their technical initiatives on the roadmap.

Ideally, what you'll hear is that it's a collaborative process. An environment in which product plans the whole roadmap without talking to other internal stakeholders and then just dumps it on engineering to build is not a good one. At best, doing things that way will miss opportunities to build products as efficiently as possible. It can also lead to an unhappy engineering team, which is a huge problem for a software company.

What are you looking for in a PM?

It's the job of a product manager to set expectations, and that requires finding out what expectations already exist first. This is a good time to understand what engineering wants out of a

PM, so you can make sure you're a good fit, sell yourself accordingly and come in on your first day knowing what people are looking to you for.

Depending on who you're talking to, you might get an engineering interviewer who isn't really sure, particularly if they're more junior. If that's the case, it's a good time to go back to the first question in this section and really dig into what their pain points are. If an engineer comes in unsure of what you're going to be doing and leaves feeling like you understand her pain points and will make it your job to address them, then you've done your job as a candidate.

What are you working on right now?

Much as I hate to stereotype, it is true that many engineers tend to be introverted, so you may find yourself getting very brief answers in response to your questions, especially big-picture ones. When that's the case, this is my go-to question. Almost everyone is comfortable talking about something they're very familiar with, so asking about the project they're currently spending hours a day working on is a great way to get the conversation going.

This should give you lots of room for follow-up questions that will get you useful information. Even something as simple as asking how things are going can be a great way to learn if the engineer is feeling good about the project and the team. Beyond that, it's always good to ask if the current project is on schedule, and if not, why not? If the answer is that the CEO demanded an overambitious timeline, that's certainly an important bit of information about how the company operates. If it's because the scope of the product increased significantly during development, then you can point out that as a PM, you'll be there to push back on scope creep in the future.

Design

A good designer is a godsend to a PM. He can take the thoughts in your head (and/or in a PRD) and translate them into designs that not only capture the functionality you need, but also add a layer of usability that makes your product a pleasure for users.

One important thing to understand about designers is that there is a difference between UX design and UI design. UI (user interface) design is probably what you think of when you think of design - it's the design of visual elements (like web pages and screens in mobile apps) that people use. It covers everything from the colors used to where the buttons go. UX (user experience) design, on the other hand, is more along the lines of what you do as a product manager - it's about understanding the journey of the user through your product. Good UX does involve some UI (if you put the buttons in all the wrong places and make them weird colors, your user will not have a good experience), but it's also a bit bigger picture, considering everything the user does, not just the visual elements of design.

Most designers can do a bit of both, but they tend to specialize over time. In early stage startups, more often than not there will only be UI designers, and it will fall to the PM team to consider the UX side of things. Either way, it's important to know who you're talking to, as your questions differ depending on which kind of designer you're talking to (and you'll come off as a better candidate if you show that you understand the difference).

Do you focus more on UI or UX?

Obviously skip this if their title is something like UX Designer, but more often than not, it won't specify. Many folks will say that they work on both - if so, ask them how they divide their time. It's rare to really have an even split, and most folks that are doing both kinds of design end up more focused on UI.

How much time do you spend with customers?

This is a question for UX designers or those who say they do both UI and UX. One of the primary responsibilities of a UX designer is to understand your users and their experiences. This can entail surveys, phone interviews, on-site product testing, group interviews with a customer advisory board and any number of other activities.

The main thing you're looking for here is to see who drives customer research. If the designers aren't spending much time with customers, then product management is going to be responsible for customer research. Generally, larger companies are the ones with dedicated UX designers. They can be a great resource for you, doing a lot of the legwork so that you can focus on building requirements. On the other hand, if you want to get into product management to work with customers, you might prefer a smaller startup where that responsibility falls to the PMs.

When do you think design should be involved in the product development process?

What you're looking for here is how much design feels ownership. Personally, I'm looking for a designer who wants to be involved as early in the process as possible, because I think having a designer thinking about a problem from the very beginning really helps to get to creative solutions. The downside to this is that if your designer is that heavily involved, they're going to have to be okay with the decisions you make, because they're going to feel ownership of the product too. If you have a great relationship, that's fine, but it can also create challenges.

For that reason, some people prefer a more segmented process, in which product is responsible for the early steps of identifying a problem, coming up with a high-level solution and then creating an initial product spec, which then goes to design to be turned into mockups.

How are design resources allocated at your company?

Lots of product managers complain about not having enough engineers, but in my experience it's always designers that are really lacking. This can be a huge challenge to your ability to do your job, so it's important to understand if you'll have adequate design resources.

There are a few potential answers to this. Designers may be assigned to product areas in the same way PMs are, so you have permanent or semi-permanent teams of one PM, one designer and six to eight engineers. This is my preference, as it ensures that the designer has all of the context around the product she's working on.

On the other hand, especially in companies with a shortage of designers, they may be allocated to projects temporarily based on their availability and the importance of a project. This means that when you need a designer, you submit a request to someone, your request gets slotted into a list somewhere based on its importance, and you get a designer when one is available. This can work well, but only if there's a good system for prioritizing requests and someone to manage it. Without those in place, designers tend to get assigned to work on requests from the person who is currently complaining most loudly that there aren't enough design resources.

At the end of the day, you should be able to get a clear explanation of the specific system of how designers are allocated, and it should be something that leaves you feeling comfortable that you'll have access to a designer when you need one.

What part of your product would you really like to redesign, but you haven't been able to?

What you're listening for here is the size and seriousness of the issues that the designer would like to fix. Every designer and PM thinks that some part of their product needs improvement but simply can't justify it. As a PM, you probably have a list of small bugs that are mildly annoying but you can never justify fixing, because they don't really cause significant issues for customers. Any designer who's been working long enough on something has a similar list - little design issues that are annoying but not important enough to fix.

If the answer you get is a bunch of little annoying issues that aren't especially serious, that's good. On the other hand, if you hear that critical pieces of the product aren't easy to use or that the designer thinks there are places where the user is having a truly bad experience, that's a red flag.

Whatever answer you get, follow up by asking why those things haven't been fixed. If little issues aren't being fixed because everyone's working on a big new feature that's top priority, that's fine. On the other hand, if those same little issues aren't getting fixed because engineering says there's actually a lot of technical complexity to them, find out why (this may require you to follow up with someone from engineering later). If you have an overengineered application that requires a lot of dev work for small changes, that should be a concern.

What are you looking for in a PM?

As with engineers, it's important to find out if the designers you're going to work with have expectations of you, and if so what they are. Use this question to dig into pain points and see where you might be able to help. If the designer leaves the room feeling like you're going to make her life easier if you get hired, she'll be your advocate when it comes time to make a hiring decision.

Product Marketing

Unfortunately, we live in an era where everyone is so bombarded with information about so many products that you can no longer believe that if you build it, they will come. Enter product marketing, whose job is to make sure that people know about the great things you're building. Since your success will likely be measured by how much people use (or pay for) your product, you should be sure that your work will be complemented by a strong marketing team.

When do you think marketing should be involved in the prod-

uct development process?

This is an interesting question because there are pros and cons to all answers. On the one hand, marketing may want to be involved very early. This makes sense - after all, they spend all day thinking about how to get customers interested in your company's products, so they'll probably have a good idea of what products people actually want. If you have marketing involved early, they'll be able to stop you from investing too much time in a product that nobody wants.

On the other hand, marketing doesn't have the same sense of the technical challenges of product development that you do, so if they're involved too heavily at too early a stage, you may end up with an overambitious product roadmap that's completely impractical.

I believe the best relationships between product and marketing have some give and take - there's input from marketing, but they know at the end of the day that the PM has the final call on what's going to be built. Some of the best product marketers I've worked with just like to be silent observers in early meetings, so that when you get close to launch, they already have a good understanding of what the product is, what features it has and what problems it is designed to solve.

Whatever the answer to this question is, make sure you feel that the folks marketing your product are ones that you can work well with.

What is the competitive landscape like?

Marketing doesn't just mean making prospective customers aware of your product, it also means making them aware of why your product is better than your competitors'. This is why competitive analysis usually falls to the marketing team. They should be able to give you a very detailed answer including who the major incumbents in the market are and which other startups are competitive.

You should have done your own research on this topic, so make sure the information you get matches what you've found. If not, ask why - if there's someone you see as a competitor that they don't, you might be misunderstanding their product (and if so, you may have a case of bad marketing on your hands).

Dig in on one or two major competitors - how is your company's product stronger than theirs, and how is it weaker? How does marketing explain the difference in their messaging? Do they feel that the product team is doing a good job of addressing the right parts of the product to ensure that it's staying competitive?

This is good opportunity not only to evaluate marketing, but also the company itself. If they can't convince you that they're a strong player in their competitive landscape, then you may want to avoid working there.

Walk me through your last product launch.

The goal here is to get a concrete idea of how marketing operates when it comes to new product launches. You should make sure to dig into both the marketing tactics they used as well as the process.

As you hear about marketing tactics, ask about why they chose what they did. If they just put out a press release and threw a bunch of money at Google Ads with no idea why, that's a problem. A good marketer should be able to tell you how each part of their marketing strategy contributes to the whole. He should understand who is being targeted and why the methods they've selected are their right ways to reach their audience. He should be thinking carefully about tradeoffs between cost and reach.

On the process side, find out when marketing became involved and what their timelines looked like. Did they have adequate time to ensure that designers and copywriters could produce good collateral, or did they find out about the product launch a week before and throw some stuff together?

You should expect a structured, thorough answer to this question, and as you dig deeper into the reasoning behind the marketing decisions, you should get well-informed answers. If you find yourself really excited about the idea of working with this marketer on your next product launch, that's a great sign.

Hiring Manager

Generally, this will be someone in product management that you will report to if hired - a group PM, director or VP. If it's anyone else, make sure there's a good reason (e.g. I was hired as the first PM at a startup, so the COO was the hiring manager as there was no director/VP of PM yet). You've probably already spoken to this person on a phone screen, but if not then you should also refer to the questions in that section of the book.

When it comes to your future boss, you really want to understand two things. First, would you want to work with them? This is someone who will have a tremendous impact not only on your career, but also your quality of life. You're going to be spending many hours every day with them, so you should be comfortable that you have compatible personalities.

Second, what are their expectations for you? At the end of the day, this is the person who is going to determine whether you're successful at your job. You should be on the same page about what success means from the beginning, otherwise you're going to be unhappy when it's time for a performance review.

Why did you join this company?

This is a good one to ask to anyone, not just the hiring manager (if you'll recall, I suggested asking it to your recruiter during the very first phone screen).

When you ask this, you're looking to find out about the person's values - did they join because the product relates to their interests, because they think the company is going to be successful, because they've worked with other people there before, or some other reason entirely?

Use the answer to this to reflect on whether your potential future boss is someone whose values align with yours. If they're focused on the profitability of the company and its potential in the market, while you're much more concerned with the company's mission, that may lead you to have conflicting views on what products to build down the line.

Whatever the answer is, I really hope to hear some excitement when answering this question. If the hiring manager is new at the company, they should definitely have the enthusiasm of someone starting fresh. Even if they're a long-time veteran of the company, though, they should be able to reflect positively on how the company has delivered on the reasons they joined (e.g. if they joined because they support the company's mission of helping people, they should be excited to talk about how many people the company has helped since they started).

Talk to me about a time one of your reports made a serious mistake and how you dealt with it.

If they've been a manager long enough, they shouldn't struggle to come up with an answer to this, so a long pause before answering may indicate inexperience.

The key thing to look for here is where they put the responsibility. A manager is ultimately responsible for the actions of their team, and that goes doubly so for mistakes. What you're looking to hear is that the manager helped to get the problem resolved then used it as a teaching opportunity for the employee who made a mistake.

Listen carefully to the language used - if it's nothing but positive words about the manager's handling of the situation and negativity at the person who made the mistake, you can probably guess how things are going to go if you do something wrong.

The manager should also have some thoughts on their own role in causing the problem. Maybe after the fact they implemented more frequent check-ins with the employee to make sure things are getting on track, or they asked another more senior member of the team to provide some mentorship. Whatever it is, you want a manager that looks inward whenever anyone on their team makes a mistake.

Let's say I end up working for you. One year from now, what should I have accomplished to make you feel like I was an excellent hire?

In most roles, it makes sense to ask about what success looks like. After all, it's tough to know if you're going to be able to succeed at a job unless you know what understand what success looks like. I like this particular phrasing of the question because it really forces the hiring manager to give a specific answers. I've tried similar questions like "What does success look like in this role?" - unfortunately, you tend to get pretty generic answers about being a leader, managing a roadmap well, dealing with obstacles, etc.

There is no right answer to this, but whatever the answer is should align with your understanding of the job. If you're interviewing for an Associate Product Manager job, the answer might be that you've taken so much work off of the plate of the PM that you're working with that by the end of your first year, she was able to manage two products. It might be that you've successfully launched a new product (or maybe it's two or three). If you're looking at an internal tools PM job, it might be that you've increased the efficiency of the company's customer support team by 25% based on the number of tickets they close per day. Whatever it is, it should be specific, and if it's not, you should keep pushing. If your potential future manager can't even define what success is for the role in specific terms, then you're going to have an extremely tough time being successful.

CONCLUSION

We've covered a lot of material here - what PMs do, how many different kinds there are, where to find companies to apply to, interview questions plus homework and more. The fact that there's this much to cover should be a good reminder of what you're getting into when you take on a PM job. You'll be responsible for a whole lot of things, from talking to customers to writing product specs to keeping your executive team in the loop on engineering's progress.

Product management can be profoundly frustrating and difficult, but at the right company it can be incredibly rewarding. You get to really understand (and drive) how your company makes products from start to finish. There are few other jobs that have the breadth of product manager, so it's something that I especially recommend to folks earlier in their career - even if you decide being a PM isn't for you, you'll have been exposed to sales, marketing, engineering, customer support and just about everything else, so you'll be able to make an informed decision about what to do next.

You may find that it's not easy to get that first PM job (or if you're lucky, you'll stumble into the perfect PM role right away, but don't count on it), so your search may require perseverance. If you talk to ten product managers, you'll find that they broke into product management in ten different ways.

I hope you've found this book to be a helpful resource. If you've finished it, and you still aren't sure whether you're ready to start trying to find a PM job, I definitely recommend talking to PMs. We really do tend to be friendly, approachable people, because so much of the job revolves around interacting with other people. If you walk over to where your company's product team sits and offer to buy anyone coffee if they'll let you pick their brain about their job, you'll almost certainly have some takers.

I've had people reach out to me to ask about my experience through LinkedIn, through my school's alumni network and through friends of friends. I've always been happy to chat with any of them, and I've ended up helping a couple of them to get their first PM jobs. It really can be tough to find great candidates, especially for more junior PM roles, so when a thoughtful, intelligent person proactively approaches me, I'm almost always happy to refer them for a job.

If you have questions, comments or thoughts on this book, please don't hesitate to email me at alexwillen@gmail.com. I would also be eternally grateful if you would leave a review on Amazon - reviews really do make all the difference when it comes to selling copies of this book.

Thanks, and congrats and starting your journey into product management!

GLOSSARY

Here are a few terms that I've used throughout this book that will be valuable to know as a product manager:

Enterprise: A large company. The definition of this will vary by what type of company you're working at and what customers it sells to. Software startups that are selling to smaller companies may define those with 500 or more employees as enterprises, while large, established companies might define them as having over 5000 employees.

Enterprise is also used to define a category of software. Enterprise software companies are those that sell to businesses (e.g. Salesforce, Microsoft). The alternative are consumer software companies like Facebook and Google.

Funnel: A set of steps that users must go through between the beginning of a process and the end of it. For example, a signup funnel may require the user to enter their email address, then to enter a password, then to reenter that password, then to click okay, then to click a link in a confirmation email they receive. Funnel analysis involves looking at what percent of users who start the funnel go on to complete it, and of those who don't, how many drop off at each step of the funnel.

IC: Individual contributor. A person who does not have any employees reporting to them.

KPI: Key performance indicator. KPIs are metrics that are used to see if something is succeeding. KPIs for a new product might be how many people use it, how much money it makes or how many users who try it once come back to use it a second time. KPIs usually exist throughout all departments of a company, not just product management.

Mockup: An early visual design of a product or feature. The quality of mockups may vary from a sketch on a whiteboard to a high-fidelity image created by a designer.

OKR: Objectives and key results. OKRs are a system in which a company creates high level objectives, usually on a quarterly basis. Departments and teams then determine which work to do that quarter based on what contributes best to the OKRs.

PRD/Product Spec: PRD stands for product requirements document. It is the main document in which a product manager defines the features and functionality of a product or feature. Every company will have some version of this document, but they may be referred to by other names like product specs.

SMB: Small and medium business. Generally this is on the other end from enterprise. Where enterprises are the largest category of customer a company sells to, SMBs will be the smallest. As with enterprises, the definition of SMB can vary - it could be a company with under 50, 100, or 500 employees.

Stakeholder: Someone who has some interest in the outcome of a product. If you're at an enterprise software company, your sales department will usually be a stakeholder in your work, because they have to sell it (as will marketing, because they have to market it). Generally, stakeholders are the people from across the company (and possibly outside of the company) that you need to keep informed during product development.

UI: User interface. The UI is how the user uses your product. Your laptop's UI includes a screen for displaying information and a keyboard and mouse for entering information.

UX: User experience. The general experience a user has while using your product. Where UI is a set of controls, UX is what a user actually does. For example, the power button on your laptop is part of the UI, but the process of pressing it in order to turn your computer on is the UX.

Wireframe: A type of mockup that is relatively low-fidelity. It typically only consists of black lines on a white background that are designed to generally illustrate where things are supposed to fit in the UI.

www.ingramcontent.com/pod-product-compliance
Lightning Source LLC
Chambersburg PA
CBHW021819170526
45157CB00007B/2651